SAINTS AND SOMALIS

SAINTS AND SOMALIS

Popular Islam in A Clan-based Society

I.M. LEWIS

The Red Sea Press, Inc.
Publishers & Distributors of Third World Books

11-D Princess Road  P. O. Box 48
Lawrenceville, NJ 08648 Asmara, ERITREA

Publishers & Distributors of Third World Books

11-D Princess Road   P. O. Box 48
Lawrenceville, NJ 08648   Asmara, ERITREA

Copyright © I. M. Lewis
First Red Sea Press, Inc. edition 1998

Typeset in Zapf Calligraphic by Books Unlimited

Library of Congress Cataloging-in-Publication Data

Lewis, I. M.
      Saints and Somalis : popular Islam in a clan-based society / I.M.
Lewis.
      p.   cm.
    Includes bibliographical references (p.   ) and index.
    ISBN 1-56902-102-3 (hardbound). -- ISBN 1-56902-103-1 (pbk.)
    1. Islam--Somalia. 2. Sufism--Somalia. 3. Somalia--Social life
and customs.   I. Title.
BP64.S6L48 1998
297.3'9'096773--dc21   98-46317
                                                                   CIP

Published in the United Kingdom by:

HAAN Associates Publishing
P.O. Box 607
London SW16 1EB

The Saints of God Speak the Same Language
Awliyo Alla iyadaa is af taqaan
Somali Proverb

CONTENTS

Contents

ACKNOWLEDGEMENTS

Chapter I is based on 'Sufism in Somaliland: a Study in Tribal Islam I and II', *Bulletin School of Oriental and African Studies*, 1955, xvii/3, 1956, xviii/1.

Chapter II was written specially for this volume.

Chapter III is a revised version of 'Some Aspects of the Literate Tradition in Somalia', in J. Goody, (ed.),*The Development of Literacy*, Cambridge University Press,1968.

Chapter IV is based on 'Shaikhs and Warriors in Somaliland' in Dieterlen, G. and Fortes, M. (eds.) *African Systems of Thought*, Oxford University Press, 1965.

Chapter V is a revised version of 'From Nomadism to Cultivation: the expansion of political solidarity', in Kaberry, P. and Douglas, M. (eds.) *Man in Africa*, Tavistock Press, 1969.

Chapter VI was originally delivered at the Third International Congress of Somali Studies, Rome and published in the *Proceedings* of the conference, ed. Annarita Puglielli, Rome 1988.

Chapter VII is based on 'Shaikh Aw Barkhadle: the Blessed Saint of N. Somaliland', *Proceedings of the Third International Conference of Ethiopian Studies, Addis Ababa, 1966*, 1969.

Chapter VIII first appeared as 'The Western Somali Liberation Front (WSLF) and the legacy of Sheikh Hussein of Bale', in J.Tubiana (ed.) *Modern Ethiopia*, A.A. Balkema, Rotterdam, 1980.

Chapter IX is a revised version of 'Spirit possession in Northern Somaliland' in Beattie, J. and Middleton, J. (eds.), *Spirit Mediumship and Society in Africa*, 1969.

Appendix I originally appeared under the same title in *Bulletin School of Oriental and African Studies, 1959, xxii.*

Appendix II was previously published under the same title in *Sudanic Africa*, vol. 5, 1994.

NOTE ON ORTHOGRAPHY:

In transcribing Somali and Arabic words in this book, long vowels are represented by doubling: *aa, ee, ii, oo, uu*. The Cushitic and Arabic aspirant *h*, and the Somali post-alveolar plosive *d* are not specifically designated since Somali and Arabic speakers will recognise where they occur without special letters being used. Place names are usually left in the form in which they occur on maps in general use.

PREFACE

This collection of essays, mostly previously published and now rather inaccessible, has two principal aims. It seeks first to bring together in a single volume the ethnographic material I have collected on various, characteristic features of Somali Islam. These focus on the cult of different types of saint and the mystical power generally attributed to holymen in Somali culture, such 'priestcraft' being, however, also the subject of deep scepticism. These studies, which include consideration of the attribution of less positive (but nevertheless empowering) spiritual force to women generally and to minority specialist craft groups, are supplemented by appendices which provide additional documentation. Perhaps the most important of these is the annotated catalogue of Arabic manuscript sources on Somali Islam, which I collected during my fieldwork and published jointly with B.W. Andrzejewski just before his death in 1994.

Secondly, and no doubt of greater interest to the non-specialist reader, this analysis of Somali Islam is also addressed to the ongoing debate on the social implications of saints' cults (not only in Islam) and their structural determinants. More generally, and in company with my earlier comparative volume (Lewis,1996), these essays are intended as a contribution to the cross-cultural sociological analysis of religion.

The order of chapters retraces the first phases of my safaris into the Somali world in as much as it begins, in chapter 1, amongst the dusty library books and papers where I began my studies, and then proceeds in subsequent chapters to the results of my own first-hand field research. This began in 1955-57, three years before independence in Somaliland and Somalia, and continued in a long series of subsequent visits up to 1992 when ill-health prevented further fieldwork in the Horn. The papers assembled here thus span a period of over forty years and have been lightly edited for mutual consistency. In particular, I have altered some of the terminology used to designate Somali social units (especially in chapter 1) to conform with my nomenclature in later writing, informed by my own field research. Chapter 1, thus, I hope benefits from this hindsight.

In the political context of the turbulent years following the overthrow of Mahammad Siyad Barre's tyrannical rule, I must emphasise that I use the term 'Somalia' here loosely to refer to the territory comprised within the former state of that name, and without prejudice to however many separate, federal, or other political units Somalis may eventually decide to create. This is, thus, in no sense designed to belittle the Republic declared in Somaliland in 1991 for whose positive achievements I have nothing but admiration. In fact, I use the term 'Somaliland' here when referring to the colonial situation, or when it is the most direct way of distinguishing this northwestern region in its present format from the rest of Somalia.

Throughout, I refer to 'Somali Islam' quite deliberately. Somalis have a markedly proprietorial attitude towards 'their' faith (sometimes referring to it as 'Somali custom'), and a universal religion here, as elsewhere, has its own local emphases and special features. Perhaps the most fundamental tension, in the past as today, in Somali Islam is that between mystically mediated views of man's relation to the Prophet and to God, and more ritualistic interpretations which deny the efficacy and propriety of such human mediation with the divine. Thus Sufism – and correspondingly, criticism of this mystical understanding of Islam – looms large here and provides the main focus of this book. As the opening, and library-based, chapter argues, Sufism is particularly well-adapted to Somali social organisation since it enables Somalis (and they are the active agents here) to sacralise their society at all levels of segmentation by indiscriminately canonising their lineage ancestors as 'saints', whatever the latters' actual religious comportment may have been. Hence, the production of hagiologies (in Arabic and Somali) celebrating these ancestral figures is an important local industry for men of learning (see examples in appendix II). check this To a significant extent, this cult of saints seems also to be in general harmony with the pre-Islamic beliefs of the Somali. But that is more speculative and is not my main argument.

Subsequent chapters record my experience of the local practise of Islam. Chapter 2, written specially for this volume, explores how the veneration of saints fits into the overall practise of Islam as I witnessed it at the local level. The extent to which this requires a reading knowledge of Arabic, the status of this language as 'holy writ', and the role of its specialist exponents, *wadaad's* (holymen), as opposed to the general laiety of 'warriors' is further considered in chapters 3 and 4. Chapter 5 examines how, in the celebration of clan identity amongst the southern agro-pastoralist Rahanwiin and Digil clans, the cult of lineage ancestor saints is replaced by local rain-making rites. Local saints generally, indeed, become more important as sources of blessing and benediction than one's own lineage ancestors, and the ideal distinction between 'men of God' and 'warrior' laiety is less sharply drawn. I argue that these differences – between the pattern of northern pastoralist Islam and that of the southern cultivators – reflect these ecological and economic contrasts.

As we shall see, in addition to contemporary living saints, there are in Somali Islam four types of saints whose mortal lives are over, but who are very much alive spiritually. In order of numerical importance, there are first eponymous ancestor 'saints', canonised and venerated by their descendants by virtue of their position as lineage and clan founders. Their descendants do not claim (nor would such claim be acknowledged) any special mystical powers (e.g. *baraka*) on account of their ancestry. Typical examples at the macro level to whom we refer in this book are the Daarood and Isaaq families of clans descended respectively from 'Sheikhs' Daarood and Isaaq.

Secondly, there are, however, other lineages which are regarded (by themselves and others) as descendants of a *bona fide* saint. Such descendants constitute a specialised line of holymen, possessing in various degree the blessed mystical properties of their eponymous ancestor: they are, in effect, living saints, however untutored they may actually be in religious knowledge and literacy in Arabic. The Reer Sheikh Muumin, named after their saintly ancestor, whose specialised powers include crop protection, are a typical example and the subject of chapter 6.

Thirdly, and certainly among the most powerful and widely venerated, are international, Pan-Islamic saints drawn from the wider Muslim calendar of saints. They are, of course, revered not for the number and power of their descendants, but for their tried and tested (and attested) religious virtues. As we see in chapter 2, their cult has been absorbed into the Somali religious calendar and they are also geographically localised at shrines, where their apparitions have appeared.

Finally, our fourth category consists of local Somali saints, who are not lineage ancestors, but are venerated for their personal reputations for piety and religious blessing. These range from local figures who are not known widely, to nationally famous saints whose shrines are important centres of pilgrimage which are compared directly with the holy sites in Mecca itself. Outstanding examples are the 'Blessed Saint', Yuusuf al-Kawnayn (chapter 7), whose shrine is in Somaliland but whose fame, as an early proselytiser of the faith and exponent of Somalised Arabic, extends far into southern Somalia. Sharif Yuusuf's lack of descendants in comparison with the prolific Sheikh Isaaq is seen by Somalis as amply compensated for by his outstanding mystical power.

Sheikh Husseen of Bale (chapter 8) in the region of southern Ethiopia adjoining Somalia, where Somalis and Oromos meet and fuse under the banner of Islam, similarly has no significant agnatic descendants of his own but is an equivalently important figure. On the southern marches of the Somali culture area, his shrine has, historically, immense political significance as a symbol of multi-ethnic Muslim identity on the edges of the Ethiopian Christian state. His multifaceted cult takes many forms, including the placation of 'holy spirits' which possess women in the region and are seen as manifestations of the saint. Here, we enter the counterpart world of spirits and jinns (chapter 9) which present the morally ambiguous face of the full Islamic cosmos of mystical powers and forces. For the saints have their direct spiritual counterparts, of a more sinister nature, in the form of 'holy spirits' or sprites whose attentions can seriously endanger the health of mortals. But such marginal forces can also empower those they particularly possess – women for example, at the expense of the dominant male world of 'devout' Muslims (for here as elsewhere, Islam is strongly gendered). The stock male response to these female afflictions is Islamic exorcism as men seek to expel what women may prefer to accommodate. (I only began to appreciate the full social implications of this after I had written the article on which this chapter is based. See Lewis, 1971/1989; 1986/1996).

To students of Somali culture and society there is one theme here which, I think, merits special attention. In the wake of the collapse of the Somali state in 1990 and with the associated upsurge of clan and local particularism by politicians of all sorts, it became fashionable for some Somali 'intellectuals'(as those with University education tend to identify themselves) – and for those non-Somali 'Somaliists' who base their understanding of Somali cultural and social processes primarily on these sources – to proclaim the cultural diversity and heterogeneity of the Somali scene. Local diversity within the Somali world has, of course, always been recognised, and indeed explored, by serious scholars. But the segmentary swing of identity between centripetal and centrifugal forces – between disunity and cohesion – is never absolute, and has always shifted historically according to the wider (political) circumstances of the Somali people (who are correspondingly more or less inclusive). I hope, therefore, that the essays on aspects of Islam in this book reveal in interesting and sometimes unexpected ways, the interrelations between different local traditions and cultural variations within the commonality of Somali Islam. The saints, like Islam, have a tendency to be ubiquitous, and the crucial role played by men of God of southern Somali origin in the general history of Somali Islam may surprise some readers of these pages.

In presenting the Sufi cult of saints as an especially appropriate vehicle for what would otherwise be an elaborate lineage ancestor cult, I hasten to add that I do not endorse Ernest Gellner's theory that the cult of mediatory saints is a product of rural illiteracy and ignorance (Gellner, 1981, pp.21ff, p.160). Literacy, the ambiguous force of which in Somali society I discuss in chapter 3, far from being a precondition for the absence of Sufism, as Gellner sometimes maintains, is an essential requirement for its creation and development here, locally, as much as in the great historical centres of learning in the Muslim world. Gellner's interpretation relates to his fieldwork among the Berbers of Morocco, and is of Sufi 'maraboutism', where he is dealing essentially with a widely scattered saintly lineage whose members play a mediatory role as marabouts among their lay neighbours. They are not all 'saints' in a strong literal sense, but rather 'holymen' by descent from a saint. As we have seen, genetically endowed saints of this type exist also in Somalia but are not the most common example of saintliness.

In fact, although Gellner's theory appears to refer directly only to this type of Berber saint, in Morocco and North Africa generally, we can readily find the whole gamut of types of saint that we have already distinguished in Somalia. Indeed, especially on the coast, many local saints are venerated as heroic martyrs who lost their lives fighting for their faith against crusading Christians (Westermarck, 1916, p.15). As far as I am aware, few if any local Somali saints are venerated for these reasons. It may thus be significant that the outstanding figure who could qualify as a holy martyr in the struggle against Christian infiltration, Sheikh Mahammed 'Abdille Hassan (see chapter 2) is *not* generally regarded as a saint. It might consequently be argued, perhaps, that such North African saints derive their miracle-working powers from their historical role at the violent interface between Muslim and non-Muslim, whereas the canonised lineage saints who are numerically most common in the Somali world reflect the internal, and often violent, dynamics of Somali society.

Ernest Gellner was not of course the first theorist to present this misleading picture of the cult of saints as the work of unsophisticated illiterate tribesmen, or peasants. In Christianity, this in fact is the traditional view, regularly urged by Church authorities and historians down the centuries. But, as the historian Peter Brown (1981) has elegantly and vigorously argued, the cult of saints in Latin Christianity was far from being the product of peasant ignorance. It was indeed, he claims, a deliberate construction of the religious elite designed to manipulate and control the masses.

In this debate on the formation of popular saints Gellner tends, although not consistently, to confuse producers and consumers. That the cult of saints, here in an Islamic context, thrives amongst people, rural or urban, who have most need of mystical succour and reassurance is not really in dispute. Nor is it at all unreasonable that, in seeking powerful intercessors, those remote from secular power should approach the problem of gaining access on the same principle, through their personal connections with those better-placed in the chain of spiritual power. Supplicants, thus, proceed in their search for succour on the principle which a close Somali friend described as governing preferment and promotion under Siyad - Barre's regime: 'It's not what you know that matters, but who you know'. This view of spiritual intercession, proceeding from the close to the remote and based on a hierarchy of client relationships mirroring secular relations, seems particularly appropriate to the political conditions of North African societies (see Eickelman, 1978, pp.161-162; 1981, pp.228-236). In the fiercely egalitarian circumstances of pastoral Somali society, the principle of client-mediated hierarchy is not strongly developed, although it is not totally foreign to their culture.

Be that as it may, the point here is that these consumers of the benefits of saintly intervention are, normally, not the inventors of Sufi mysticism. Historically, as has been amply demonstrated by historians of Islam, Sufism is essentially the work of sophisticated and highly literate urban men of learning and thrives as successfully amongst their less fortunate fellow townsmen (and townswomen) as amongst rural populations. Urban Islam itself, is of course, far from the mode of sober legalistic orthodoxy ('puritanism' as opposed to 'Catholicism' in Gellner's terminology) depicted by Gellner. As E.W. Lane's (1860/1908) celebrated classic study of life in late nineteenth century Cairo long ago established, the practise of urban Islam includes a rich spectrum of exotic beliefs in spirits, the evil eye, magic, astrology and geomancy.

Urban religious literacy, thus, is not only dedicated to the production of learned commentaries on the Koran by the orthodox doctors of Islam. It also includes a vast out-pouring of texts on magic and astrology which circulate widely in and from centres of religious excellence. Often, paradoxically, as with the exponents of other ideological orthodoxies, the most learned members of the intellectual elite engage in this parallel religious traffic. As it diffuses more generally as a literate medium, Islam is thus in practise a multilayered package which includes a host of disparate (and partly unorthodox) elements. It is typically *not* the religion of the Book, but the religion of the books (cf. Lewis, 1996, pp.139-154). These marginal and potentially anti-Islamic forces are strikingly illustrated in the Somali context in the form of the spirit possession afflictions to which women are particularly prone (chapter 9).

The mystical power of holymen and saints in this essentially warrior society is, I argue (chapters 4 and 5), ideologically consistent with a wider distinction that Somalis draw – in ideal terms of course – between secular power based on superior force ('might is right') and the counterbalancing spiritual power of the politically weak. This is part of the ideal contrast (in many contexts, as I emphasise, eroded in practise) between holymen or 'men of God' (*wadaads*), and warriors (*waranleh*) – literally 'spear-bearers'.

In this connexion, it is significant as I mention in the opening chapters (and as Cerulli long ago recorded) that a number of the leading local Somali saints as well as the leaders of religious settlements are men whom Somalis consider to be of lowly origin since they do not belong to politically important clans or lineages. But this is not generally the case, and while in a general way it makes sense to say that, given the belligerent lives of most men there is ample scope for pacificatory men of God, it is emphatically not the case (as Douglas, 1966, p.110 argues in a rather crudely deteministic way) that such holymen typically belong to marginal lineages. The point is that, as we have seen in our classification of saints, not all sanctity is embodied in particular groups or lineages. Just as some saints are free-standing individuals and not canonised as lineage founders, others – probably the majority of holymen – are so regarded in an achieved individual, rather than agnatically ascribed capacity. Moreover, as we discuss in chapter 7, the traditionally despised craftsmen, especially the least numerous and least powerful in secular terms, are also endowed with a mystical aura, albeit negatively charged. But, *pace* Douglas, they do not play a vital role in the general social process.

I would like, finally, to pay tribute to some of my masters in this field of study. First, the great Italian scholars, Massimo Colucci and

Enrico Cerulli, the latter in particular in his voluminous works on Somali culture and language unquestionably laid the foundations of Somali Studies. Would that all those who aspire to follow in his footsteps were as accurate and meticulous in scholarship. On a number of occasions, Somali acquaintances told me how much better he spoke their language than I did. Secondly, my own friend and colleague, the brilliant Somali linguist and Polish poet, B.W. Andrzejewski who died in December 1994. Finally, my most enlightening and patient teachers of Somali life and culture, of whom I mention only a handful here: Muse Galal, Yusuf Meygag Samatar, Sheikh Aw Jama Umar Ise (inadvertently also my pupil, since he started his own research in oral history after witnessing my efforts in the bush), and Dr. 'Abdillahi Deriye (who in 1957, when we worked together in Hargeisa, had just completed secondary school). My anthropological field research in Somaliland and Somalia was financed first by the Colonial Social Science Research Council, then by the Carnegie Trust and the British Academy. I also continued my research while working on development projects for FAO, USAID, ODA, Action Aid, UNHCR and various other organisations to all of whom I am grateful for their support of my work (whether deliberate, or involuntary). In putting these papers together, in this form, I have benefited from the help of Ms. Benedetta Rossi which was made possible by a small grant from the staff research fund at LSE.

I.M. Lewis
London School of Economics, January 1998.

Chapter 1

APPROPRIATING MYSTICAL ISLAM TO SACRALISE THE SOCIAL ORDER

In a Muslim culture, the study of Islam tends to throw as much light on the social structure as the study of the social structure does upon religion. The close interdependence here has always been particularly clear in Muslim societies with a state-like structure where the Shariah (the religious law in the widest sense) has had a wide field of application, although, of course, with the progressive Westernisation of the Islamic world the gap between the spiritual and temporal realms is again widening (cf. Gibb, 1947; Milliot, 1949; Fakhry, 1954). But the conformity of social and religious structure is equally far-reaching in an uncentralised Muslim society although it may not at first sight appear so. Somali society is a case in point. This essay explores, in a preliminary way, the role of Sufism in the social structure of the Somali and is, at the same time, designed to elucidate the nature and function of Somali genealogies.

THE ETHNIC CONTEXT

It is unnecessary here to justify the ethnic classification 'South-Eastern Cushitic' which embraces the Somali, Afar, Saho, Oromo, and Beja, and which rests upon similarities in material and social culture, including religion, and upon physical and linguistic affinities, and certainly in the case of the first four, upon traditions of common origin. I assume here that the pre-Islamic religion of the Somali was that of a Cushitic 'Sky God' (*Waaq*), and that the present Muslim structure of Somali society owes much to the interpretation of Islam in terms of Cushitic beliefs. It follows that it should be possible to relate the social functions of present-day Somali Sufism to syncretism between the two religions. In interpreting Cushitic belief

among the Somali, the wider literature describing the religion of the
Afar, Saho, and Oromo has been drawn upon, but I do not deduce
from Cushitic religion in general any belief or custom for whose
independent existence among the Somali there is not reasonable
evidence. It is not implied that all those features of Somali social
structure whose interaction with Islam is considered are necessarily
typically Cushitic, but simply that in the pre-Islamic state of Somali
society they were related to Cushitic institutions.

We shall deal particularly with Sufism and examine the way in
which its social organization, political, and religious structure are
associated with the *baraka* of Sufi sheikhs, and their personal genealogies which trace religious power to the lineage of the Prophet
Mahammad. It will be argued that the genealogical canalization of
divine grace (*baraka*), dependent upon connections with Mahammad's clan of Quraysh, finds close parallels in the social and religious significance of Somali clan genealogies (*abtirsiinyo*). These
similarities between Sufi genealogies, and genealogies in the traditional (pre-Islamic) social order help to explain the ease with which
Somali genealogies are Arabized, and are a significant factor in the
Somali claim to descent from the Prophet. Such an interpretation, it
will be noticed, does not depend upon the validity of the preceding
assumptions on the nature of Cushitic religion, but, since these seem
well established it is relevant to consider the incorporation of Sufi
genealogies into the Somali lineage structure in relation to them.
The religious aspects of Somali genealogies which centre in sacrifice
at the tombs of eponymous ancestors were, in the pre-Islamic state
of Somali society, intrinsically a part of Cushitic religion, and knowledge of the larger hierarchy of Cushitic spirit-refractions does, I
think, throw light upon the nature of sacrifice to the dead, and leads
to some elucidation of the religious meanings attached to Somali
genealogies. Thus, it is proposed (i) that Sufi genealogies are
adopted due to the close resemblances in their religious and political
functions to Somali clan genealogies, and (ii) that this assimilation
corresponds to underlying similarities in the Cushitic and Sufi religious concepts which attach to genealogies.

THE SOCIAL SETTING

In the 1950s when this research began, the Somali population was
estimated at about two to three million*, distributed in the territories

---

*Estimates in the 1990s, after years of conflict and the emigration of
thousands of refugees, still remain extremely approximate but suggest a total
population of six to eight million.

of French, British and ex-Italian Somalia (the UN Trusteeship Territory administered by Italy), the south-eastern dependencies of Ethiopia (the Ogaden), and the Northern Frontier Province of Kenya. The Somali were (and are) largely nomadic pastoralists, owning in abundance sheep, goats, cattle, and camels used for milking and the transport of the nomad's tent and possessions. Some temporary cultivation is practiced, and in some areas, permanent cultivation especially in the southern riverine region. Here arable land occurs along and between the courses of the two rivers which water southern Somalia (the Shabelle and Juba). Here enclaved settlements of Bantu and others are engaged in permanent farming, and some Somali clans, especially those of the Digil-Mirifle (and Rahanwiin) clan-family have adopted a sedentary or semi-sedentary mode of life. Mixed farming is characteristic of this region, and there is an increasing tendency for nomadism and transhumance to give place to fixed cultivation.

The Somali nation comprises two main divisions, the 'Soomaali' ('Saamaale') and 'Sab'. The Sab Digil-Rahanwiin tribes form an extensive wedge of cultivators between the rivers of Somalia and separate the nomads of northern Somaliland from those of the south. The 'Soomaali', who are numerically superior, despise the 'Sab' for their sedentary way of life, for their mixed origins (Oromo and Bantu admixture is pronounced), and for their mixed genealogies. Nevertheless, Sab are included in the designation 'Soomaali' by outsiders, in much the same way, it seems, as the inhabitants of the British Isles are frequently indiscriminately referred to as 'English'. Within the Somali nation, Soomaali and Sab are differentiated although in the 1950s there was an increasing tendency for the Soomaali-Sab cleavage to be ignored in the rising tide of Somali nationalism. Urbanized and Westernized Somali maintained that discrimination was 'old-fashioned', contrary to the injunctions of the Prophet, and that it undermined the unity of the Somali people. In practice and actual social relations, however, these ideals are often betrayed, which serves to indicate how deeply ingrained the traditional Somali social order is. Still, the cleavage remains the primary subdivision of the Somali nation[1], and in the rest of this paper. I shall use the term 'Somali' to include the Sab except where a distinction is expressly stated[2]. Each comprises a vast segmentary system of units which may be classified as: 'clan families' (of which there are six; Dir, Hawiye (and 'Pre-Hawiye'), Isaaq, Daarood, Digil, and Rahanwiin), confederacies, sub-confederacies, clans, and lineages.

The clan stands out as a clearly defined unit which embraces the most generally effective social solidarity. Livestock-theft and war characterize the relations between clans, and interclan hostility is frequently of long standing. Internally the clan tends to be divided by feud amongst its fractions. Within the clan, however, homicide is normally settled peaceably by payment of blood-compensation. With the extended enforcement of the European administrative system, clans were also, whenever possible, obliged to settle their differences by payment of compensation in place of further fighting. The obligations entailed by clan membership are clearly formulated in the procedure for the adoption of strangers,[3] who undertake to share responsibility in payment and receipt of blood-price and inother matters. In essence, the clan is ideologically of one blood, and it is, in short, a social, territorial, political, and to some extent religious unit closely similar to that of the Nuer 'tribe' (Evans-Pritchard, 1940) or of the Arab Bedouin (Jaussen, 1948). It is not, however, entirely exogamous. Like the total Somali society of which it is the microcosm, the clan comprises a balanced system of sections of various orders of segmentation. But in most cases there are at least four levels of segmentation, for some clans boast as many as 100,000 members. The average, however, seems to be about 20,000 members.

In each political unit from the basic group of closely related families to the clan confederacy, the elders constitute a council representative of the group's interests and convened by a political figurehead. In the tradition of the medieval period when the petty Muslim sultanates of southern Eritrea and north-western Ethiopia engaged Christian Ethiopia in war, such 'chiefs' were styled both by the Somali and by the foreign administrations as 'Sultan'. But this title does not imply that its incumbents wield authority over a centralized state, and is not to be understood in the classical Muslim sense.[4] Usually the clan recognizes a ceremonial chieftain (called variously *boqor, garaad, ugaas*), as president of the clan council. Yet, not every clan owns a common leader. In effect, a chief's authority derives from the structural situation – from the circumstances of clan allegiance – and fluctuates with it. (The role of chief, as I discovered in my subsequent field research, is more developed among the southern cultivators than among the nomadic pastoralists (see Lewis, 1961, 1994, Ch. 6; see also below Ch. 5).

Considerable religious power may attach to such a leader (especially amongst the Digil and Rahanwiin). In the past, the role seems to have been connected with rainmaking, and there is evidence that this function is still retained amongst some groups in the north-west corner of Somaliland and of certain parts of Somalia. In many cases, the leader still conducts periodical rainmaking ceremonies (*roobdoon* 'seeking rain') and the rite performed in Somalia to mark the onset of the main rains. The chief's glance is referred to as 'the burning eye' (*il kulul*) and is so strong that, among some closely related clans it was apparently usual for a visiting leader to avoid a face to face encounter with his equivalent and to be greeted indirectly by a representative. Consequent upon his special relation with God, such a leader might call down blessing or misfortune upon his people and their stock (or so the literature reports).

From the structural point of view, his most important function was, however, to preside at the commemorative ceremonies which are held at the tombs of the eponymous clan ancestors. Each lineage celebrates its founder at his shrine, offering up its own particular form of sacrifice[5] (Cerulli. 1923, p.7). Where a hereditary leader is recognized, members of his family (called *Gob*) represent him at sacrifices performed by the heads of subsidiary clan fractions. In the case of clan confederacies with a chiefly lineage the same procedure is followed in the ceremonies of component groups. It is this duty more than any other which establishes the sanctity of a hereditary chief, for when he represents his people in sacrifice at the eponymous ancestor's shrine, it is his own lineal ancestor whom he commemorates before God. He, the living representative of the founding ancestors, is the closest descendant of those whom he celebrates on behalf of his clan. Generations later, he in his turn will be regarded as an eponymous founder and will be commemorated in sacrifice by his descendants on behalf of their clansmen. In the traditional accounts of war and migration (especially in southern Somalia), it is often the religious aspects of leadership which are singled out and held to be responsible for the success of one group at the expense of another. The fortunes of war are to some extent regarded as a reflection of ritual efficacy.

On the political side again, there is no specifically constituted police organization to enforce the decisions which are arrived at by the 'chief' in council, except of course in the small sultanates, which have remained a legacy from earlier times in some parts of Somalia (Cerulli, 1919. pp. 40 ff.)

The Somali Lineage System

The emphasis placed upon descent has already been indicated. The key to any understanding of Somali social structure lies in the meaning of genealogies (*abtirsiinyo*). The total genealogical tree of the Somali nation represents the potential unity of all its component parts: clan-families, confederacies, clans, and clan segments. Social propinquity is expressed in terms of agnatic kinship. The relations between groups of every order are in the genealogical idiom expressed as relations between eponymous ancestors. This is the principle which Somalis assume to underlie social relationships. The basis of political action is the agnatic lineage system – its religious significance relates to the eponymous ancestors to which it refers, and who are celebrated in the sacrifices performed at their tombs. Such is the traditional social system, associated with nomadism, and preserved where nomadism still prevails.

In the south, however, where sedentary cultivation is replacing nomadism, the relations between territorial groups are not always expressible in terms of descent.

The process of change is gradual; at first territorial units form having a mixed clan or lineage structure in which the political unit is coordinated with a dominant clan or lineage. With subsequent development, and the continued settlement on the same territorial unit of increasing numbers of immigrants of heterogeneous clan origin, the agnatic lineage structure becomes more distorted, and the segmentation of the dominant lineage may no longer represent territorial distribution. But it usually continues to have political functions. This is particularly characteristic of the agricultural tribes of the Sab family. It is important, however, to observe that although the characteristic territorial unit of these regions is an agricultural settlement or 'mixed-village', agnatic kinship may still be applied at a higher level to describe the relations between larger territorial aggregates.

There are, as has been mentioned, six clan-families – Dir, Hawiye (and 'Pre-Hawiye'), Daarood, and Isaaq in the 'Soomaali' group; and Digil and Rahanwiin in the 'Sab'. The Isaaq and Daarood clan families are represented as descending from their Arabian founders' marriages with Dir women in the early years of the spread of Islam among the Somali (cf. Lewis, 1955; 1994, pp.95-112).

Traditions of Arabian descent are especially strong amongst the Isaaq and Daarood, but are held independently by the Hawiye and Dir and even by many of the Sab tribes who, as it happens, have as bold claims to Arabian descent as their northern Somali neighbours (the Dir, Isaaq, Daarood, and Hawiye). All clan-families can establish connections with each other without going as far back as the Prophet's lineage, but the breach between 'Soomaali' and 'Sab' is only bridged by tracing descent to the Qurayshitic line of Mahammad. Only at this level of inclusiveness are the Soomaali and Sab joined as the two branches of the Somali nation, and it is in this context especially that the Somali consider themselves the children of the

Prophet. For this solidarity transcends all sectional interests and divisions, including that between Soomaali and Sab, and represents a real consciousness of common nationality and religion. Individual genealogies (*abtirsiinyo*) trace ascent through the hierarchy of social units from the smallest lineage to the clan family, through the primary bifurcation of Soomaali–Sab, through the Prophet's descendants, and culminate finally in Mahammad, although they often extend beyond to include the Prophet's ancestors and resemble typical Arabian genealogies (cf. Wustenfeld, 1853). Usually Somali genealogies are imperfectly Arabized (Islamized) and contain a mixture of Cushitic and Arabic names indicative of the absorption of Arab genealogies. Unless, however, Somalis wish to emphasise their exclusiveness with respect to other peoples, that is when only relations between Somali are in question, the genealogies given stop at Soomaali or Sab and comprise between 22 and 30 names. At their greatest extension, genealogies representing political and religious connection are drawn out beyond the clan-family eponyms to embrace the Prophet and his lineage.

ISLAM

Relations With Arabia: The Introduction Of Islam

The historical foundations of the contemporary claim to descent from the Prophet lie in the existence of relations between Somaliland and Arabia from the earliest times. Migration from and to Arabia has always been and still is a constant feature of Somali life. There has always been a considerable floating population of Arabs in various stages of absorption among the Somali. Moreover, there is little doubt that Islam reached the Somali Coast shortly after the Hejira when its establishment is recorded by Arab writers of the 9th and 10th centuries. The coastal commercial colonies which had been founded by the Himyarite Kingdom before Islam eventually developed into the small Muslim states of Zeila (in its widest extension known as Adal) in Somaliland, and of Mogadishu in Somalia. These were ruled by local dynasties of Somalized Arabs or Arabized Somalis. The history of Zeila has been described by Trimingham (1952, pp. 58 ff.) and need be no more than summarized here. Cerulli's research (Cerulli, 1924, 1926, 1927) shows that from the beginning of the 9th until halfway through the 13th century, Mogadishu was functioning as a trading colony which comprised a federation of Arabian tribes. Persians also played some part in the early history. The Arab settlers had elected chiefs and acknowledged the religious and jural authority of one lineage, the Qabtan ibn Wa'il. In the course of time Somali influence increased, and from a loose federation of Arab-Somali peoples a sultanate with a local dynasty (the Muzaffar) emerged in the 13th century; by this time Shangani and Hamarwein, the two halves of the town of Mogadishu, were firmly established and Hamarwein was dominant.

This dynasty survived into the 16th century when the sultanate declined as a commercial centre, and reverted to a hegemony of small townships. At the time, Mogadishu was under pressure from tribes of the Hawiye clan family who were advancing southwards through Somalia.

By the second half of the 18th century, Somalis had gained control of Shangani and imposed their imam as ruler of Mogadishu. Portuguese and British colonization contributed to the final collapse of the sultanate. In the 17th century the city had been occupied by the Imam of Oman for a short space, and remained after his withdrawal in vague dependence to him. With the division of the Muscat State early in the 19th century, Mogadishu was allotted to the Sultan of Zanzibar, who attempted to secure a more binding dependence by establishing military garrisons along the coast. Almost immediately after, these were sold to Italy, and Mogadishu became part of the Italian colony of Somalia.

Southern Ethiopia supplied Zeila with its trade and the town reached its greatest heights in the 14th century, but began to decline after Ahmed Granhe's (known to Somalis as Guray – the 'left-handed') celebrated campaigns against Christian Ethiopia in the 16th century. Its history was from the beginning the chronicle of a series of wars against the Ethiopian 'infidels' (Christians) waged in alliance with the other petty Muslim states of southern Eritrea and north-eastern Ethiopia. Mogadishu, as we have seen, had a shorter period of prosperity in the 14th century, and then declined fairly rapidly under the joint pressure of nomadic incursions from the interior and the influence of external colonization. Such centres as these had an important effect in the development of Islam among the Somali. With the Arabian colonies firmly entrenched in the other trading ports, they provided a foothold from which Islam spread amongst the nomads of the interior.

Sufism among the Somali

The Somali are orthodox Sunnis and adherents of the Shafi'ite rite of the Shariah. Sufism is long established and well developed; the remainder of this chapter seeks to explore its role in Somali society.

As is well-known, this revitalizing current arose in Islam between the 9th and the 10th centuries, attaining in its classical form its aesthetic and theological climax in the 12th and 13th centuries. True Sufism is considered by some authorities to have fallen into decadence in this century (Arberry, 1950). Amongst the Somali, after a period of great activity and general expansion up till the 1930s, the Dervish movement seems to be on the wane, although, from my library sources in 1952 it was extremely difficult to assess its contemporary importance. (This is what subsequent chapters seek to establish on the basis of my field research). Elsewhere, Sufism has always tended to form a conservative barrier against European administration, and many of its adherents have strongly opposed the extension of education lest it should undermine their authority. The hostility, real or imagined, of colonial regimes has reinforced the esoteric and clandestine character of Sufi practice in colonial territories and made it all the more difficult to estimate its true significance. However, it is not difficult to determine its importance in the social structure of Somali society, for whatever its present number of adherents, it has left an indelible impression.

Generally, the adherents of Sufism belong to the congregations or communities, in many Muslim countries known as *zawiya*, amongst the Somali as *jama'a*, of the various Orders (*tariiqa* , 'The Way') each with its distinctive doctrines and services (*dhikri*). *Tariiqa* means 'path' in the sense of the Way to follow in the search for righteousness, and the Way to God. The spiritual goal of the *tariiqa* is *ma'rifa*, absorption in God (gnosis). Those who have traveled furthest, through virtue, the practice of devotion, and the grace which God has vouchsafed them are nearest Him. As the Path is traversed, successive steps of the way are demarcated as 'stations' or 'states'. These are discussed below. For his godliness and virtue the founder of each Order is held to be closer to the Prophet and so to God, exemplifying in his teaching and life the True Path which it behoves the zealous to follow. The founder is a guide who through his particular qualities of devotion, and by his special virtue including the grace (*baraka*) bestowed upon him by God, leads his disciples towards God. His *baraka* passes to those who follow in his Path and dedicate their lives to his example. Each Order is distinguished by the specific discipline which its founder has established as the True Path. Since there is no God but Allah and Mahammad is His Prophet, religious prestige is connected with the Prophet's Qurayshitic lineage. Thus, those in whose blood (recorded in personal genealogies) the Prophet's grace (*baraka*) flows, are eminently suitable for election to the office of *khalifa*, head of an Order or of sheikh, head of a congregation. Sheikhs and *khalifas*, as also the founders of the Orders themselves, have personal genealogies tracing descent from ancestors connected with the Prophet Mahammad.

To what extent such claims are historically true is in the present context irrelevant. The tradition is that descent from Quraysh entitles to religious office and that to be a Sufi sheikh or *khalifa* implies such descent. Thus in their fullest extension the personal genealogies of the founders of Orders and their local representatives, sheikhs and *khalifas*, reach back to the Prophet's lineage. According to the lineage principle, in terms of which relationships among the Somali are understood, each *jama'a* is identified with the genealogy of the *khalifa* or sheikh. The consequences of this in the total genealogical structure of Somali society will shortly be seen. Within each *tariiqa* the authority for the incumbent of the office of regional *khalifa* is founded upon a chain of tradition which has two branches. Unlike his personal genealogy, these attach to the office, not to the person. The *silsilat al-baraka* (chain of benediction) traces the chain of grace which unfolds from the founder of the Order through his successive disciples down to the present incumbent of the office of *khalifa*. The *silsilat al-wird*, the other branch, connects the founder with the Prophet, and, through his mediation, with Allah. The *silsilat* (lit. 'chain') consists of a list of names through which spiritual affiliation is traced and in some ways resembles a genealogy. It is quite separate, however, from the sheikh's personal genealogy although that also is regarded as endowed with power.

In initiation (*wird*), the covenant (*'abd*) for the *tariiqa* is administered to the novice by the head of the community in a formal ceremony at which the service (*dhikri*) pertaining to the Order is celebrated (for a description, see Robecchi-Bricchetti, 1899, p. 423; Trimingham, 1952, p. 237). The novice swears to accept the *khalifa* as his guide and spiritual director through the *baraka* of the founder. He is then instructed in the performance of prayer-tasks (called variously *awrad*, *ahzab*, and *rawatib*), and is provided with a prayer-mat to carry upon his shoulder, a vessel for ablution, and a rosary (*tusbah*) to finger as he recites his prayers. Somali *tariiqas*, apparently, are characterized by fewer stages in the novice's progress towards illumination than were customary in classical Sufism (see on this point, Arberry, 1959, pp. 74 ff.). At first the novice is styled 'aspirant' (*murid*) but also referred to by his brethren (*'ikhwan*) as 'brother'. The majority of initiates never proceed beyond this stage. *Qutb*, which is the next step, requires a certain degree of mystical perfection but is not comparable to the *qutb* of literary Sufism. Each successive step becomes increasingly difficult, and *al-wasil* the next grade, signifying union with God after long strife (i.e. the attainment of gnosis), corresponds to induction to the leadership of a fraternity. *Al-maddad*, the final goal, is attained by few pilgrims indeed, for it is that reached usually only by the founders of the Orders themselves. Membership of the community does not imply celibacy; adherents live with their families in the community. In some regions, women were reported to have their own *tariiqas* where they participated in the services in the name of the Prophet's daughter, Fatima, whom they regarded as the founder of women's Orders. Female adherents were veiled (the veil is not usually worn by Somali women), and are generally more amply clad than other Somali women. But for them also there was no embargo on marriage.

There are always many people who although not formally admitted to an Order and not living in the community, follow the public ceremonies while ignorant of their esoteric content. Acknowledging the piety and religious powers of the founder whom they venerate as a saint, they regularly call upon his followers whom they regard as similarly endowed to act as mediators in disputes. Many of the brethren thus fulfil the functions of kadis and this is one of the many ways in which the sphere of interest of the Sufi community encroaches upon that of the tribal structure. Clansmen may turn to the head of the *jama'a* for assistance and counsel, to the neglect of the clan leaders. This is one instance of a wide and far-reaching conflict between Sufism on the one hand, and the clan organization on the other which we shall consider in some detail below.

SUFI BROTHERHOODS

The three most prominent *tariiqas* among the Somali are in the order of their introduction, the Qaadiriya, the Ahmadiya, and the Saalihiya. The Rifa'iya *tariiqa* is represented amongst Arab settlers but is not widely distributed or important. In the south the Order's main centres are the coastal towns of Mogadishu and Merka; there are also some adherents in Somaliland. The Qaadiriya, the oldest Sufi Order in Islam, was introduced into Harar in the 15th century by Sharif Abu Bakr ibn Abd Allah al-'Aydarus (known as al-Qutb ar-Rabbani: 'The Divine Axis'), who died in 1508 or 1509 (AH 914). Abu Bakr is probably the best known Shafi'ite saint in southern Arabia where he is called al-'Adani[6] and his mosque is the most famous in Aden.[7] The Qaadiriya became the official Order of Harar and has considerable influence in the surrounding country. To the south, the Order does not appear to have acquired much importance in the interior of Somalia until the beginning of the 19th century when the settlement of Bardera (known locally as *jamaha*), had become established on the Juba river. The Qaadiriya has a high reputation for orthodoxy, is on the whole literary rather than propagandist, and is said to maintain a higher standard of Islamic instruction than its rivals. The Ahmadiya, and the derivative Saalihiya, were both introduced into southern Somalia towards the close of the last century, although the Ahmadiya may have entered Somaliland somewhat earlier. This Order was founded by Sayyid Ahmad ibn Idris al-Fasi (1760-1837) of Mecca and brought to Somalia by Sheikh 'Ali Maye Durogbe of Merka. Mahammad ibn Saalih, in 1887, founded the Saalihiya as an offshoot of the Rashidiya founded by Ahmad ibn Idris's pupil Ibrahim al-Rashid (Cerulli, 1923, pp. 11, 12; Trimingham, 1952, pp. 235-6; see also document 22 in Appendix II).

The principal Saalihiya proselytizer in Somalia was Sheikh Mahammad Guled, a former slave, who launched the Order there by the foundation of a community among the Shidle (a Bantu people occupying the mid-reaches of the Shabelle river, see Lewis, 1955, p.41). Mahammad Guled died in 1918 and his tomb is at Misra (named after Cairo, *Misra* in Somali), one of the communities which he had established among the Shidle. The Order's stronghold is in Somalia but there are some communities in Somaliland. According to Cerulli (op. cit., pp. 14, 18) the Saalihiya is strongly propagandist, but less sophisticated than the Qaadiriya in mysticism and teaching. In the past it has been closely associated with Somali nationalism. The best-known anti-colonial rebellion was that led by Mahammad b. 'Abd Allah (born about 1865) of the Habr Suleman Ogaadeen clan, who made several pilgrimages to Mecca (1890-9), and joining the Saalihiya, sought to attract the northern Somali to this Order. He founded several communities and in 1895 proclaimed himself *khalifa* designate in Somaliland. By 1899 he was hailed as Mahdi (although he repudiated this title) and initiated the jihad against all 'infidels'. He was repudiated by the leader of the Saalihiya in Mecca, and from 1900 to 1904 British forces along with, from time to time, half-hearted Ethiopian and nominal Italian support, conducted four major campaigns against him. His power was continually reduced but the rebellion was never decisively crushed, and it dragged on until 1920 when the Sheikh Mahammad died. (For the results of more recent research on the life and times of this remarkable figure, see Lewis, 1988 chapter 4; Samatar, 1982; 1992; Umar Iise, 1974, 1976; Keenadiid 1984; Sheikh-Abdi,1993.)

The Ahmadiya, with the smallest number of adherents of the three Orders, is said to concentrate more on teaching than the Saalihiya (Cerulli, 1923, pp. 12 ff.). Both Orders are for the most part distributed in cultivating villages along the two rivers of Somalia, and in the fertile land between them. Qaadiriya congregations, on the other hand, are more usually dispersed and do not form autonomous settlements of cultivators. This, naturally, is particularly the case in the north where there is little arable land.

Where the congregation forms a stable cultivating settlement, the land, which has been acquired through adoption into a host tribe, is the collective property of the community and is divided among the affiliates by their sheikh. Continuity of tenure depends upon the maintenance of satisfactory relations with the clan of adoption and the regular fulfilment of the various obligations which adoption imposes. Tenure is precarious and is in theory at any time revocable. It follows that the individual holdings obtained by affiliates are not automatically inheritable; absolute rights to land or crops are never obtained by members of the community. If a member leaves he relinquishes all rights to his holding and probably his crops also, although he may sometimes be allowed a portion of the harvest. The fields are worked collectively so that the harvest in each brother's holding represents the collective labour of the community. Part of the harvest is used to maintain the funds of the *jama'a*, which also depend upon gifts and payments for ritual or religious services performed by affiliates. Liabilities met from these general funds consist of aid to the poor, assistance of pilgrims to Mecca, and expenses connected with missionary work and the various dues payable to the clan of adoption. As far as the latter is concerned, the *jama'a* acts as a clan section subject to the same privileges and duties as are other sections of the clan. Congregations act as training centres for the local men of religion (*wadaad*),[8] usually described as 'bush teachers' or 'bush preachers', who wander from camp to camp through the bush, stopping now and then to hold classes where at least some rudimentary knowledge of theology is imparted. In these transitory bush schools children are taught prayers and verses from the Koran and generally acquire the ability to read and write some Arabic. Children who attend regularly receive a thorough grounding in the Koran, and their familiarity with Koranic texts remains with them throughout their lives.

Wadaads are also important as acting in the capacity of unofficial kadis administering the Shariah to the extent that its competence is recognized, i.e. in matrimonial affairs, inheritance of property, contract, mortgage, etc., and assessment of the requisite compensation for injuries. In interclan politics, they have little authority to award decisions, and where their recommendations conflict with clan interests they are normally ignored, for *wadaads* here act as mediators rather than as arbitrators. It is probably through the *wadaads* who issue from the *jama'a* communities that Sufism exerts its greatest influence in Somali social structure. The parent communities themselves are essentially centres of mystical devotion, and have produced a considerable Arab-Somali religious literature written mainly in Arabic (but in some cases in Somali transcribed in an adaptation of Arabic script).[9] It is probable also that Sufi words are to be found in Somali oral literature, and research should be directed to discovering to what extent this is the case (see in this connection Abdisalan Yassin Mahammad, 1977). Mysticism is adopted as a means to union with God (gnosis); Somali Sufistic literature treats of divine ecstacy and appears to be similar to Sufi writing in general. An interesting example is an unpublished manuscript called *tawassul ash-shaikh Awes* (Uways) written by Sheikh Uways[10] which consists of a collection of songs for *dhikri*. Where such works are biographical, as for example in the autobiography of Sheikh 'Ali Maye Durogbe,[11] they are likely to contain an account of the author's justification to claim descent from Quraysh. Almost all such works include a section in which the author's claims to Qurayshitic descent are set forth. Perhaps the most important Somali Sufi writing is a collection of works compiled by Haaji 'Abdullahi Yusif published under the title *al-majmu'at al-mubaraka*.[12] Haaji 'Abdullahi of the Qaadiriya *tariiqa* was a member of a group of sheikhs (known as Ashraaf), attached to the Majeerteen tribe of the Daarood clan family; his work is analyzed by Cerulli (1923, pp. 13-4, 22-5).

The Cult of Saints

An important feature of the Sufi communities lies in the extent to which their founders are venerated. The local founders of Orders and congregations (*jama'a*) are often sanctified after their death. Their veneration gives rise to cults which rival the devotion due to the true founder of the *tariiqa* and even of the Prophet Mahammad. Their tombs become shrines, tended by a small body of followers or the descendants of the sheikh and those who have inherited his *baraka*. To the shrines come the members of the Order as well as local tribesmen who are not initiates, to make sacrifice as occasion demands, and to take part in the annual pilgrimage to the shrine of the saint on the anniversary of his death. Outstanding events in his life are similarly celebrated. Muslim saint-days which have no connection with indigenous saints are unpopular especially in the interior. But to the extent to which the Qaadiriya Order is followed, emphasis has been given to the saint-day (*mawliid*) of the founder al-Jiilaani, although even this festival enjoys only limited observance. Saints are not always associated with a particular congregation or Order. Many are ubiquitous, and being common to several Orders share the same veneration within the religion of the country. They are venerated for particular qualities. One of the most popular in Somalia, Saint Aw Hiltir (a name suggestive of non-Islamic origin) is regarded as the protector of man from the attacks of crocodiles; another, Saint Aw Mad, is recognized by tribes of the Rahanwiin clan family as the guardian of the harvest.

Tombs are scattered all over Somalia and many, apparently, commemorate pre-Islamic figures who have been assimilated in Islam. Some of the families acting as the custodians of their ancestors' shrines have developed into small clans, usually dispersed; others have lost all autonomy and are scattered as holymen (*wadaads*), proselytizing and teaching. Others again remain attached to a particular clan as the holders of a hereditary office of kadi. Such, for example, is the case with the seven lineages of the Gasar Gudde tribe of Lugh in Somalia, where the office of 'chief' rotates among six lineages, while that of kadi is invested in the seventh, the Reer Dulka Madow (Ferrandi, 1903, pp. 213, 262 ff.; Lewis, 1955, p.115).

This represents one of the possible conclusions in the history of a saintly family attached initially to a tribe in clientship, where the religious group has worked its way into the lineage structure of the tribe and established a permanent position. A good example of a dispersed clan venerated for their *baraka* are the Reer Sheikh Muumin whose ancestor's shrine is at Bur Hakaba among the Elai of southern Somalia. Their influence extends throughout the entire Rahanwiin tribal-family and tribute is paid to them on account of their reputation as sorcerers (Ferrandi, 1903, pp. 138-9, 242-3). Ferrandi describes them unflatteringly as a 'gang of robbers' implicated in cattle raiding and profiting by their ancestor's sanctity to impress and exploit ignorant people (see further below, Ch. 6). A similar dispersed sheikhly group are the Aw Qutub of Somaliland whom Burton (1894, I, p.193) described as the descendants of Aw Qutb ibn Faqih 'Umar who was then claimed to have crossed from the Hejaz 'ten generations ago' and to have settled with his six sons in Somaliland. The Aw Qutub are widely scattered and are found as far south as the Ogaden. They have the title 'Sheikhaash' which Burton translates 'reverend'. In fact, such families of Arabian origin are found all over Somalia and are often rapidly assimilated in the Somali social structure where their members enjoy high prestige (cf. Cerulli, 1926).

THE ROLE OF SUFISM IN THE SOCIAL STRUCTURE

We may now consider the position held by Sufi *tariiqas* and congregations of communities in the social structure. It is obvious that for the total social structure, the fraternities provide potential channels of alliance amongst warring clans separated by the very nature of the clan. For the communities, economic and political entities though they may be, and often themselves at enmity even within the same Order, are bound together through community of religious purpose. They aim at the development and diffusion of Islam. Such were the ideals so successfully translated into a transcendental movement ignoring the narrow bonds of tribalism by the Saalihiye jihad-leader Haaji Mahammad b. Abd Allah. His campaign is an illustration of the potentialities which the *tariiqa* organization offers for the extension of national unity when a sufficiently great figure emerges to inspire such feeling. As elsewhere in Islam, the new urban political parties seem to have their roots in the *tariiqa* organization and to be a development from it.[13] Trans-clan nationalist aspirations which previously found some outlet in it were later promoted by political associations, the strongest of which was the Somali Youth League (SYL). Within the clan structure individual communities exercise considerable influence, and it is this aspect of their social functions which I wish particularly to consider. As we have seen, among the nomads and especially in the north where there is little or no arable land, communities cannot generally form cultivating settlements as they do in the less barren south. They cannot therefore so easily exist as independent autonomous local groups. Among the southern cultivating tribes (the Sab), settled cultivating communities occupy an interstitial position on the ground. As social entities they are accordingly in a better position to develop into units independent of clan allegiance and to play a mediatory role in the social structure.

This naturally has important consequences in the lineage structure. To take an example: The Qaadiriya community of Bardera was founded on the Juba River at the end of the 18th century by a Rahanwiin clansman, Sheikh Ibrahim Hassan Yabarow (see Cassanelli, 1982, pp 135-146). New settlements quickly sprang up round the mother community. The affiliates were faced with considerable hostility from the surrounding tribes. They fought the Oromo Borana, the Gasar Gudde (Somali Rahanwiin) who were successfully defeated and their centre Lugh-Ferrandi‡ destroyed, and, finally,

---

‡ Italian colonial name, later changed to Lugh Ganaane.

the people of Bardera extended their sway to the coast subjecting the villages of Baidoa, Molimad, and the coastal town of Brava. Thus they established dominion over all tribes of the Rahanwiin clan family. Retribution, however, was to follow. The Rahanwiin recovered strength under the leadership of the Sultan of the Geledi (then a powerful Rahanwiin clan), and after a series of battles besieged and destroyed Bardera in 1843. For some years Bardera lay deserted but began to rise again with the foundation of a new community by Sheikh Mahammad Edan of the Elai. By 1924 it was possible for Colucci (1924, p.264) to describe the new centre in the following terms: 'The settlements of Bardera constitute a truly independent territorial group freed from all adherence to the tribes from whom the original grants of land were obtained'.

Adoption

All communities originally enter the clan structure through an act of adoption. Genealogically this implies incorporation into lineage. Colucci (1924, pp.78 ff.) has drawn attention to the frequent occurrence in clan genealogies of names signifying 'holy', 'religious', 'saintly', etc., which denote the attachment to clan units of Sufi communities or groups of holymen celebrated for their *baraka*. The fact that some clan families, especially those with particularly stong traditions of Arabian descent such as the Isaaq and Daarood of northern Somaliland are often referred to as *'haaji'* or *'haashya'*[14] indicates that they are in some sense regarded as sanctified. This is an illustration of the extent to which religion is identified with clan structure among the northern nomads. We shall return to this point later. In the genealogies of the southern cultivating clans (the Sab), however, such words tend to occur in the lower portions of clan genealogies. Sometimes their occurrence indicates fairly feeble ties of attachment between adopting tribe and priestly section. In other cases where the attachment is more tenuous these titles represent extraneous aggregates often of long standing. As examples of dispersed clans of holymen we have already considered the Reer Sheikh Muumin (see also chapter 6) among the Rahanwiin and the Reer Aw Qutub of Somaliland. Both are typical representatives of this class. The Sheikhaal Lobogge section of the Herab clan of Somalia are, on the other hand, a good example of a religious group or community firmly assimilated to the clan of adoption. Sheikh Lobogge, the eponymous ancestor of the group, is a descendant of Sheikh Sa'ad whose tomb is at Geledi in Somalia. Groups which have not achieved such firm integration in the clan structure, or assimilation in the lineage structure, are the

Ashraaf among the Saraman clan cluster,[15] the Walamogge among the Elai,[16] and the Waaqbarre among the Dabarre clan.

The Ashraaf are described as rising to power in a manner typical of such groups; they acted as mediators in a series of disputes amongst the Saraman tribes which concluded in the expulsion of one, the Haraw, and the division of another, the Lisan (Leysan), into two new clans, the Lisan Horsi and the Lisan Barre. At Saraman, the Ashraaf are known as the 'Three Feet' and take part in clan councils as arbitrators and peace-makers. There are many religious clans known as Ashraaf in Somaliland, and no doubt some of them derive ultimately from immigrant Ashraaf. In view of the importance of Mogadishu as a centre in the diffusion of Islam it may well be that the Sharifs in the Shanghani quarter of Mogadishu who are of the Ba Alawi clan of Hadramaut,[17] and who settled in Somalia in the 17th century, may constitute one of the original nuclei from which Ashraaf blood has spread.

The Walamogge wield considerable influence in Elai politics through the high prestige which they enjoy as men of religion. They claim to have accompanied the Elai in their wanderings before they reached their present territory, but they only recently became the official sheikhs of the Elai after they had ousted another religious group – the Reer Fogi (or Reer Faqi). The founder is said to be of Oromo Arussi origin, but as in the case of all religious sections they have vague traditions of descent from Quraysh which they exploit to the full. The Walamogge have considerable autonomy and are segmented into primary, secondary, and tertiary divisions (Colucci, 1924, p.141).

The Waaqbarre, who are attached to the Dabarre tribe, comprise three sections and have mixed traditions of connection with the Oromo Arussi and descent from a 'Great Arabian Sheikh'.

As is clear from the foregoing, many *tariiqa* communities develop into groups of *wadaads* (see above), clustered around the shrine of their founder. Again there is the constant factor of the immigration of Arabian religious groups and their Somali descendants who may have no direct affiliation with a particular *tariiqa*. The complete picture is intricate and complex; it is not always possible to establish the *tariiqa* affiliation of religious groups with a Sufistic organization. Certainly it is often difficult to discover to which of the three – *tariiqa* communities, sheikhly families, or Arabian immigrants – particular names in clan genealogies actually refer. It is probable that in many cases all are confused. They have in common an association with *baraka*. It seems, however, that apart from Arabian families venerated for their name and piety and not necessarily Sufis in the strict sense, it may generally be inferred that the primary units are *tariiqa* communities. This supposition is supported by the fact that Arabian immigrants whose genealogies show connections with Quraysh and consequently endowment with *baraka* are venerated in the same manner as Sufi saints and their cults are absorbed in the over-riding *tariiqa* organization.

The land necessary for the foundation of a *jama'a* is sometimes made readily accessible through the nomad's lack of interest in and contempt for cultivation. Often it was obtained as the result of skilful intervention in clan disputes over land. Contested areas of arable land bordering clan territory were ceded to astute sheikhs who were thereby enabled to establish *jama'a*. At the same time, the creation of these farming settlements contributed to the demarcation and definition of formal clan boundaries (Lewis, 1955, pp. 43 ff., 143). Thus, for example, a chain of communities marking the principal watering place, and boundaries between clans was set up along the Shabelle River from Afgoi to Mahaddei (Cerulli, 1923, p. 26). For this reason it is appropriate to describe Sufi *jama'as* in southern Somalia as forming enclaves amongst clans and occupying an interstitial territorial position analogous to their role in inter-clan politics.

The community's lands are acquired through adoption into a host tribe. Adoption within the clan and lineage structure (if this is still funtioning) places the head of the community and his followers in the initially inferior status of clients, subservient to the clan elders and chief. At this stage the burden of the conflict between tribal custom (*heer, tastuur*) on the one hand, and the Shariah on the other, seems to lie against the Sufi community. For the members of the *jama'a* are subject to conflicting loyalties. The Islamic code which should rigorously govern their internal affairs cannot always be enforced in their relations with the clansmen upon whom they are in dependence. Should tension between clan and community reach a high pitch, the community is in danger of losing its tenancy. However, such is the strength of tradition that in the hands of a wise sheikh, skilful in the maintenance of good relations with his clan of adoption, tenancy easily lapses into ownership. Tenure has given rise to absolute possession. Rights to land may never be challenged, and the *jama'a* may achieve sufficient power to free itself completely from clan allegiance. Such was the case of Bardera (see above, p. 17).

With the high premium which the increasing adoption of agriculture has caused to be set upon land, disputes over possession are common. But rivalry over land for cultivation is only one among many likely points at issue between a Sufi community and its clan of adoption. In addition to the general disharmony between clan custom and the Shariah, the interference of sheikhs in clan politics, and the passing of religious leadership from clan to *jama'a*, customary sanctions would seem to be weakened by the asylum offered in *jama'a*s to defaulters from clan justice.

At the same time, a variety of factors encouraged, the growth of Sufi farming communities. The opportunities which a stable existence in agricultural settlements affords, together with the greater stability of clan relations among the sedentary cultivators or part-transhumant clans of Somalia, attracted dispossessed people, many of servile origin, and promoted the further development of agriculture. The soil is favourable, there was administrative encouragement to cultivate – and many settlers were by nature cultivators – and the Shariah, more thoroughly applied here, provided a code whose juridical ordinances are more appropriate to farming settlements than they are to nomadic society. All these factors contributed to the reorganisation of the lineage structure, as well as to the formation of *jama'a* farms. It is not surprising that there seems to have been a constant drift towards the religious settlements and away from the clans; that it was no greater was probably partly due to the nomad's contempt of cultivation.

When these factors are considered it is clear that there are many opportunities for friction between clan and adopted community. In all disputes the procedure followed is the same; the clan claiming the land occupied by the community seeks to abrogate the mandate by which it is alleged to have been ceded. The conflicts which ensued were usually resolved by the intervention of the administration. A typical example of the type of dispute likely to arise is the following: in 1920 the Hawadle claimed the land which the community of Bardere occupied and which, it was maintained, had been granted to the community thirty-eight years previously. The clan held that the grant had been only provisional, and that the ground was now required for its own use, especially since several Hawadle families had already settled in the lands of the *jama'a*. As the head of the *jama'a* continued to ignore their requests, clansmen continued to move into the community's lands without admission to the Order. The Sheikh was then moved to protest to the Italian Administration, claiming that the disputed lands had been obtained not from the Hawadle but from an adjacent clan, the Baddi Addo. The case was solved by the government's forcing those Hawadle who had illegally joined the community to withdraw after the harvest of their crops. Sufism triumphed and the community's rights were upheld against those of the clan. The position of *jama'a*s was further strengthened by the Italian administration's policy of appointing official kadis from the ranks of Sufi brethren (*wadaads*) (Cerulli, 1923, pp.28-9, 32-4). But government policy does not always seem to have been consistently on the side of the Orders, and has doubtless frequently turned disputes between clans and religious Orders to its own advantage.[18]

We have noted how the difference in ecology between the northern terrain occupied by nomads and the southern occupied by semi-nomads and sedentary cultivators, governs the territorial disposition of *jama'as*. There is naturally a higher proportion of permanent agricultural Sufi settlements in the south than in the north, and consequently a higher proportion of autonomous communities freed from direct clan dependence. In the south, *jama'as* occupy an interstitial position in the social structure parallel to their territorial distribution.

Genealogical Assimilation

We have seen how Quraysh is the symbol of divine grace and how the genealogies of Sufi sheikhs and *khalifas* vaunt connection with the Prophet's lineage. We have also seen how in the client status, and thus at some point in the history of every *jama'a*, the community is identified with its head and with his genealogy. The incorporation of such genealogies seems to have contributed to the process by which the Somali nation has come to trace descent from the Qurayshitic lineage of the Prophet. The Orders as they today exist in Somalia do not date from before the 15th century (the time of the introduction of the Qaadiriya), but it is unlikely that they could have assumed their present constitution and strength without some earlier proto-*tariiqa* organization (cf. the development of Sufism in Morocco, Drague, 1951, pp. 9-117). It appears probable, therefore, that the Qurayshitic pattern of Somali genealogies may have developed in step with the formal emergence of the Orders in Somalia. As emphasized earlier, *tariiqas* are not alone responsible for the introduction of Qurayshitic genealogies. Many of the immigrant Arabs who established chiefly dynasties among the Somali, and who naturally brought their Arabian genealogies with them, were doubtless not all Sufis themselves. Nevertheless, it is significant that the Somali celebrate as the founders of their faith, and venerate in the same fashion as they do Sufi saints, figures such as Sheikhs Isaaq and Daarood – who if not themselves historical personages – are certainly the types of such (cf. Lewis, 1994, Ch. 4).

Sociologically, it thus appears that the claim of descent from Quraysh is the necessary outcome of the application of the Somali lineage principle to the part played in their social structure by Islam generally and by Sufism in particular. This consistency is apparently facilitated by the parallel functions of Sufi and Somali genealogies. That the nomads have stronger traditions of descent from Quraysh is to be expected since, unlike the southern cultivators whose arable lands facilitate the formation of autonomous independent Sufi communities, the *jama'as* of the northern nomads are seldom self-contained and seem to be generally more closely identified with the clan structure.

THE CUSHITIC BACKGROUND

Zaar and *Waaq*

The Supreme Being of Cushitic religion is a 'Sky God' who is regarded as Father of the universe. The entire world of nature, including man and his possessions, belongs ultimately to God. The root-name for the Sky God may be *Zaar*, in Somali '*Saar*', since, according to Cerulli (1923, p. 2) *zaar* occurs in this context with only slight modifications in most Cushitic languages and is the form used among the Agao whose traditional religion has been taken as the archetype of Cushitic religion (cf. Ullendorff, 1955. pp. 63-4). Since, however, comparative study of the Cushitic languages is in its infancy, this theory is uncertain. Among the northern Somali *eebbe* (Father) is a common name for God – now Allah – and among the Hawiye of the south the word *Waaq* is often used (cf. Oromo: *Waaqa*). *Waaq* in northern Somalia occurs in certain obscure expletives but is not generally used to designate God (see appendix I). *Zaar* itself appears to occur in the form *saar*, which, as we shall see, connotes a spirit-refraction accreted to Islam as a malignant jinn. *Eebbe* and *Waaq* are now, of course, applied to Allah, and these Cushitic names and their derivatives are still found as personal and place-names.

God is apprehended as He watches over creation in the sun's light, just as man is aware of his surroundings through the gift of sight. Prayers run:

> 'Watch us God, You who have eyes, know and we shall know, for after You have known we know.
> Knowledge is Yours, sight is Yours, watch us with good eyes. Make us see well. Sight is Yours.'

The semantic relation is eyes, seeing, sun, and light. God's eternal constancy is compared to the centre-pole of the hut. 'May the centre-pole be as of iron'. Without support man's house collapses, but God, 'the same without the centre-pole', is full of wonder and power. According to Cerulli, in the 1930s, Somalis still sang : 'This Sky, the same unchanging, without the central-pole according to the Divine Will'. The Sky God's belt is the rainbow, and the rains are in his keeping as a gift for man; certain individuals have power over the rains through their relation to God.

Saar in Somali describes a state of possession by a spirit which is also called saar. The extreme symptoms are frenzy, fits, or madness, and the spirit itself is, in the Islamic setting, described as a kind of jinn whose malignant powers cause certain types of sickness. Among the eastern clans of northern Somaliland, invisible wadaads act similarly to saar but have less serious effects and are merely responsible for some minor forms of illness. Saar spirits may be expelled by persons who have acquired mastery over them. Saar are expelled in a dance which may become much of a public entertainment (see Ch.9 for a fuller account based on my field research).

The dance is widely distributed among the Cushitic peoples of north-east Africa and often the possessed dancer acts as an oracle (see Leiris, 1934). Beyond the Cushitic areas it occurs as far away as Egypt (Kahle, 1912), the Anglo-Egyptian Sudan (Trimingham, 1949, pp. 174-7), and even the Hijaz (Hurgronje, 1888-9, II, pp. 124-8). The explanation seems to be that the saar (zaar) dance and cult have spread far beyond the bounds of Cushitic culture with the export of slaves from Ethiopia where it has its Cushitic origin (Cerulli, 1933, II, p. 35; see also Lewis, Hurreiz and as-Safi, 1991).

Other Religious Concepts

The realm of the Sky God includes a multitude of subsidiary spirits; the spirits of the bush, certain animals, some snakes, scorpions, termites, and other insects frequently credited by Somali with malignant powers. In certain situations clans are described as linked to trees and animals which are addressed by maternal kinship names, but the connection does not appear to be totemic. Spirit-refractions are said to have their seats in those possessed, and, among the Cushitic Agao of Gondar in Ethiopia the spirit-ridden subject is referred as the spirit's 'horse'. A similar spirit is encountered and overcome in the crossing the threshold ceremony (kalaqaad) which marks a male child's first expedition outside his mother's hut. The baby is carried over the threshold by his mother's brother (Cerulli, 1919, p. 23). Although generally obscured by and syncreted in Islam, divining and various forms of sympathetic magic are still practised. Ordeals and oath-taking by swearing on stones are used to establish testimony. Charms and amulets, especially as prophylactics, enjoy wide popularity. Their efficacy, now, of course, depends upon association with the Holy Koran. In this context it is perhaps not irrelevant to mention the fire-kindling ceremony of *dabshid* which is widely observed and marks the commencement of the solar year. The festival is condoned in some parts of Somalia by representing it as a Muslim expiatory rite; in one district it is known as the 'feast of beating'.

In southern Somalia, death is regarded as a transformation. In the grave, the corpse lies clothed and provided with a supply of food. The dead are remembered in periodical ceremonies ('sweeping the tomb') at which livestock are slaughtered and food distributed amongst the poor, slaves and servants, and the aged. Gifts of food and clothes are sometimes offered, often in response to dreams. 'I dreamt that my father showed me his torn clothes. Here are some clothes, let him take them'. Or again, ' I have given my dead mother an ox, now my father is thin and hungry and wants something to fatten him. Here is another ox, let him come and take it'. Old men are said to be preoccupied with amassing burial wealth and, according to Cerulli, on occasion set aside as much as three-quarters of their inheritance for the performance of 'sweeping the tomb' ceremonies (remembrance rituals) after their death. Sacrifice (*Waaq da'il, rabbe barii*) plays, as we have seen, an important part in the life of the Somali. From the structural point of view its crucial form is the annual celebration held at the tombs of the founding ancestors of lineages. The assimilation within Islam of this, the most vital aspect of sacrifice in relation to the lineage system, will be discussed below.

SUFISM AND SYNCRETISM

Sufism and the Shariah

Muslim mystical theosophy may be regarded as embodying the vital and flexible spirit of Islam. Like all mysticism, Sufism concentrates on the personal relationship between the believer and God, and must be regarded by those who consider that the core of religion is to be found in an 'I–thou' relationship as the mainspring of Islam. The Shariah – the law of the Islamic community – originated in a theocracy which had transcended the bonds of tribalism, and has in its subsequent elaboration always referred (in theory at least) to a religious state. That part of the Shariah which relates only to purely ritual or religious observance applies equally well to clan or state, because it deals with the relations of the believer to God. But the sectors of the Shariah which elaborate a corpus of private and public law based upon the concept of citizenship are not applicable, save with major limitations, to a stateless clan-based society.

The ecological dichotomy reflected in the divergence between nomadism and sedentary cultivation, which as we have seen, is reflected in the two different patterns of *jama'a* organization – dependence and identification in the case of the nomads, independence from clan allegiance and less close assimilation in the case of the cultivators – operates in the same sense here. In the urban centres of the coast and in the arable lands of the south where the lineage principle is less conspicuous, the purely legal as opposed to purely religious – to make a separation which in traditional Islam is largely artificial – ordinances of the Shariah naturally have wider jurisdiction.

But amongst the nomadic Somali, the application of the Shariah tends to be restricted to intra-clan affairs and certain matters of personal status. Its relevance outside this narrow field is, of course, recognized by clansmen but is not always upheld in practice. Even within the clan, the jurisdiction of the Shariah is limited by the force of local custom (*heer, tastuur*) – not an unusual situation in the Muslim world. It is true that the recognition given to the Shariah in the British and Italian judicial systems provided an extended mechanism for the regulation of external clan relations. Thus the Shariah is one of the sources of law in the settlement of clan disputes although the case may not be heard in a kadi's court. There are, however, many *wadaads* issuing from the *tariiqas* who practise as kadis outside the governmental judicial structure. The scope of the application of the Shariah, although supported by strong religious sanctions, is limited by the power of the clan leaders. This state of affairs represented the traditional social order before the advent of the *Pax Britannica* or the *Pax Italiana*. Despite these differences in the jurisdiction allowed to the Shariah, there was little difference between the nomads and cultivators in the importance attached to the fundamental principles of Islam. Except for a few clans who have remained relatively sheltered from Muslim influence, the five 'Pillars of the Faith' – the profession of the Faith; prayers; fasting, somewhat irregularly observed perhaps; almsgiving; and pilgrimage – seem to have been universally practised in Colucci's time, as now. Competent witnesses were generally struck by the devoutness of the Somali clansman.

There is, of course, no opposition between Sufism as a movement and the schools of Muslim law, but the material reviewed here suggests that Sufi theosophy – as opposed to the Shariah – is in its basic principles particularly suited to Somali society. These principles have been firmly assimilated while what in the Shariah is inapplicable to a clan society has been largely ignored. On the other hand, various customs, which appear to have no necessary connection with the lineage system nor to be essential to nomadism, persist and resist the full application of the Shariah. On the whole, however, Somali society has interpreted Islamic institutions in the light of its own clan structure and has produced the Sufi pattern outlined. But it would be wrong to argue that because Somali clan organisation is, in the ways outlined, opposed to the application of the Shariah, the only possible response is Sufism. The difference between the theory and application of the Shariah has always been considerable, in state as well as clan society. The suitability of Sufism to the condition of Somali society is much more important than the impracticality of parts of the Shariah. We turn now to consider the adoption of Sufism in terms of the assimilation of Sufi theosophy to what is presumed to have been pre-Islamic belief.

The Nature of God and His World

Although clearly delineated with greater precision, the absolute supremacy of Allah (indicated in the believer's submission (*Islam*) to Him) closely resembles the onmipotence of the Sky God. As in the cult of *Waaq*, men are God's creatures, subject to His Will and must live in constant fear of Him and praise Him always. Similarly to *Waaq*, Allah stands at the centre of His universe as its Supreme Power and Creator. The Muslim doctrine of determinism finds its parallel in the attitude of submission and resignation in the face of *Waaq*. But Muslim fatalism is more rigidly determined and more elaborately worked out, since man's actions are predetermined and set down in the tablet which is before God, similar to that Divine Archetype from which the Koran was delivered to the Prophet. The same tendency towards a greater systematization in Islam finds expression in the much more clearly defined position of Allah in the awarding of right and punishment of evil. *Waaq* upholds right but there is little indication He does much more. Muslim eschatology accordingly strikes a new note. Death was a transformation but not to an exact equivalent of the anthropomorphic Muslim paradise. Formerly the spirits of the dead were to a certain extent localized about the sites of their tombs. We shall examine below the way in which this affects the reverence paid by Somali to the tombs of Muslim saints. Fundamentally, however, man's relation to *Waaq* closely mirrors his relation to Allah and it is hardly surprising that Somali should apply the names of the former Cushitic Sky God to Allah and call Him *eebbe* and *waaq*.

The fact that Islam is a revealed religion appears at first sight to constitute a fundamental difference between the two religions. But whereas there is apparently nothing in the cult of *Waaq* comparable to the tradition of revelation of Allah to the earlier prophets and finally to Mahammad as the 'Seal', Sufi theology has concentrated on those texts and traditions[19] referring to the immanence of God in the world and has interpreted these as justifying a continued revelation and more immediate knowledge of Allah. In Sufism, emphasis has veered from the position of the Sunna towards an interpretation of the Prophet's role as that of *logos*, and the approach to Allah has been correspondingly widened. The approach to God, first through the Prophet, and then through Sufi sheikhs and saints, finds its parallel in the association of sacrifice to *Waaq* with lineage ancestors.

Comparison of the pre-Islamic Somali spirit-world with Muslim angelology and demonology reveals again the much higher degree of systematization in the latter. In Muslim theology, angels, pre-eminent amongst whom is Gabriel, generally figure as Divine Messengers created by God to serve and worship Him. They are charged with recording man's actions in this life, receiving his soul in heaven, and acting as his counsel on the day of judgment. On the other hand, jinn are those rebellious spirits created similarly to man, but of fire in place of earth, and committed to Solomon's keeping, who seek to lead man astray and to subvert the teachings of the prophets. It is as jinn that the majority of pre-Islamic spirits previously associated with *Waaq* are assimilated in Islam. This is illustrated in the following tale reported from the Gasar Gudde clan of Somalia: 'Solomon, son of David, on whom be peace, commanded

all men, all the animals, the wind, spirits, and demons, the entire kingdom of the Great King. One day the jinns were at work as usual, and Solomon, leaning against a tree, seemed to be watching them although he gave no sign of repose. Solomon was dead, but remained supported by the tree while the jinn unaware of what had happened went on with their work. At last the termites succeeded in eating their way through Solomon's support precipitating him heavily on to the ground. The jinn quickly ran to the spot and saw that the son of David was dead. They began to rejoice for now they could stop working since their master was dead. They hastened to the termites and made a pact with them, saying, "You make your nest of earth and we will bring the water for its strengthening". From this time forth jinn and termites are in alliance' (Ferrandi, 1903, p. 309).

Here within Islam the spirits attendant upon the mysterious construction of termite mounds are associated with jinn in Solomon's
keeping. The relation spirits–termites is given Muslim sanction in
Solomon's authority over jinn. Similarly the source of the efficacy of
divination, ordeals, charms, and prophylactic amulets has been
transferred from *Waaq* to Allah when beneficent and to jinn when
mischievous or evil. Now the favourite amulet is the Sufi rosary (*tusbah*) whose ninety-nine beads remind the believer of the innumerable praise-names of Allah and help him to perform his prayer-tasks.
Perhaps equally popular as amulets are small leather pouches
armed with inscriptions from the Koran. Thus phenomena which
formerly owed their power to some connection with *Waaq* now
originate in Allah, the ultimate source of all power[20].

Saar spirits are described by Somali as a kind of jinn. The whole
spirit hierarchy of *Waaq* is being progressively Islamized. This is a
process which naturally also applies to God's attributes. Among the
Gasar Gudda, again, the rainbow, from being the Sky God's belt, has
become the path good souls take to heaven, although it is also con-
tended by some to be the smoke made by rain falling upon termite
hills. Rain-drops are believed to turn into angels (an understandable
evaluation); thunder (*uri*) is the voice of angels (*malaika*) or the noise
of their combat in striving to stop rain. Lightning (*birk*) darts forth
from the armpits of *melek Mikail*, the archangel Michael. Michael
(*Sura*, II) appears thus to be taken as a symbol of war. These are a few
examples indicative of the way in which the Muslim spirit hierarchy
seems to have been understood in terms of Cushitic cosmology.

Saar Rites and *Dhikri*

To return to the *saar* dance. It is evident that this ceremony has
inherent susceptibility to syncretism in the services (*dhikri*) of the
Sufi *tariiqas*. Especially is this true of the most popular forms of the
dhikri, where trance states in which fading or death of self, believed
to result in mystical union with God, are induced by direct stimula-
tion. The *dhikri* held by the Ahmadiya at their annual pilgrimage to
the tomb of Sheikh 'Ali Maye Durogba has been described as follows. 'Thousands come to the tomb from all parts of Somalia. The
festival lasts fifteen days and culminates in a great *dhikri* on the last
night when the pilgrims form an immense circle and, to the accompaniment of singing, recite their formulae in raucous saw-like voices
rhythmically swaying their bodies. This is reported to continue until
day-break. Once they have got well worked-up, large numbers fall
foaming to the ground in induced epileptic convulsions.'(Barile,

1935) This is neither an informed nor a sympathetic description but it serves to indicate how closely the *tariiqa dhikri* resembles the *saar* dance and suggests a syncretism which is well established in Egypt and elsewhere[21].

The similarities between the attainment of spirit possession (or the release from possession) and absorption in Allah which are the objects of the dance and the *dhikri* respectively have already been pointed out.

The Assimilation of *Baraka*

In the foregoing, various aspects of the conversion of spirit-refractions of *Waaq* to Muslim equivalents have been discussed. These are variations upon the general principle of the translation of Cushitic power into Muslim *baraka*[22]. The most fundamental application of this exchange is that underlying the absorption of Sufi gene-alogies which contributes, as I have suggested, to the inclusive ascription of the Somali people to the Qurayshitic lineage of the Prophet. It is this equivalence which permits Muslim saints to be venerated and communed with in sacrifice and prayer at the sites of former pre-Islamic shrines. These are the places which famous Somali Muslim saints are believed to have visited in their peregrinations, or at which they are believed to have appeared to believers in dreams. Tombs are scattered all over the country and more of them are places of manifestation or visitation than the actual burial places of the saints whose *baraka* is sought in pilgrimage. Thus, as in all Muslim countries, old shrines continue to command respect although the source of their power has been transferred to Islam.

The veneration of saints tombs has, however, a more specific significance since it is through sacrifice to eponymous ancestors at such local shrines that clan relations were maintained with *Waaq* at all levels of the social structure. Moreover, the emphasis placed on genealogies and the importance attached to eponymous ancestors, celebrated at their tombs, have promoted and continue to promote the adoption of Sufi genealogies and the canonisation of eponymous clan founders. Thus, within Islam the ancestors of clans and clan segments are represented as saints or sheikhs, while the whole system is validated in the attribution of Somali origins to immigrant Arabians (in the case of clan families, to figures such as Sheikhs Isaaq and Daarood). This process, in turn, has been facilitated by the immigration of Arabs down the centuries which provides the historical component in Somali traditions of descent from Arabia.

This short discussion of Cushitic religion and its Islamization has been included here to outline an ideological framework for the study of Somali and Sufi institutions. The apparent similarity of the concepts of Cushitic power, immanent in Somali genealogies, and *baraka*, immanent in Sufi genealogies (which attach to the institutions of sacrifice to founding clan ancestors and to saint veneration respectively) underlies the transfiguration of clan founders into Islamic saints. The organization of both cults depends upon a lineage system in which religious power of a similar nature inheres.

In conclusion, in this opening chapter based on library sources, I have argued that although in origin a product of the sophisticated and highly civilized centres of the Muslim world, Sufism is eminently suited to clan society. Where stress is placed upon the power of lineage ancestors to mediate between man and God, Sufism provides an interpretation of Islam which, while preserving the supreme absoluteness of Allah, modifies the uniqueness of the Prophet by interposing more accessible and more immediate intercessors.

Notes

1 This division is, as Professor R.B. Serjeant has suggested to me, reminiscient of that between the northern and southern Arabs who trace descent from Adnan and Qahtan respectively.

2 Correctly as above indicated 'Soomaali'.

3 Clients are called *magan* in the northern dialects; in the south '*arif*, and among the Digil, *sheegad*.

4 Contrast the classical definition of Ibn Khaldun, *Prolegomenes*, trs. de Slane, I, p. 382. vol. xvii. Part 3.

5 For pre-Islamic (Cushitic) terms for sacrifice see Appendix 1.

6 Professor R.B. Serjeant, personal communication.

7 See below, Chapter 4.

8 See below, Chapter 4.

9 On the subject of a suitable script for Somali see: King, J. S. 'Somali as a written language', *Indian Antiquary, August and October, 1887; Maino, M.*, '*L'alfabeto Osmania in Somalia', RSE,* 10, 1951; Galaal, M. H. I., 'Arabic script for Somali', *Islamic Quarterly,* I, 2, 1954, pp 114-8; Maino, M., *La Lingua Somala Strumento d'Insegnamente Professionale,* 1953; Andrxe-jewski, B. W., 'Some problems of Somali orthography' *Somaliland* Journal (Hargeisa), I, 1, 1954, pp. 34-47 and 1974; see also chapter 3 below.

10 See Cerulli, 1923, pp. 12, 22, who describes the sheikh as one of the most important proselytizers of the Qaadiriya in the hinterland of Somalia, although, as indicated above, the Order had already at the beginning of the 19th century assumed some prominence in the interior with the foundation of the community of Bardera on the Juba river. 'Awes' is as Somalisation of 'Uways' and the sheikh's full name is Uways ibn Mahammad al-Barawi. See further chapter 2, below.

11 See above, and Cerulli, loc. cit., p. 22.
12 The *haaji's* full name is Sh. Abd Allah ibn Yusif al-Qalanquli al-Qutbi al-Qadiri ash-Shafi il-Ash'ari. The work was published in Cairo in AH 1338 (1918-19) and printed by Mustafa al-Babi al-Halabi in two volumes. It constituted a most valuable collection of the lives of the Somali Qaadiriya sheikhs.
13 cf. Gibb, 1947, p.55.
14 See Lewis, 1955, p. 17.
15 The Saraman tribal cluster comprises the Lisan Hersi, Lisan Bari, the Reer Dumal, Garusle, Luwai, Hadama, Jiron, and the Muslim-wena (see Colucci, 1924, pp.181ff).
16 For this important Rahanwiin clan see Lewis, 1955, 36-9, 40, 121, etc.
17 Cerulli, 1927, pp. 404-6. See also Moreno, M.M., 'Il dialetto degli Asraf di Mogadiscio', *RSE*, 12, 1953, pp. 107-39.
18 According to Cerulli (1923, p. 29) the policy of the Italian Administration was to admit the leaders of *jama'as* as religious leaders, but to allow them no political authority. The development of *jama'as* in the fertile area was actively discouraged and the foundation of new settlements constrained as far as possible. In the arable lands thus protected from the further encroachment of *jama'as* the government saw the possible realization of its aim to establish the economic independence of the colony through extensive agriculture development.
19 For a readily accessible compilation of *hadiths* used by Sufis as a basis for their ascetic and theosophical interpretations of Islamic theology, see Arberry, 1950, pp.24-30. See also Ch. 2 below.
20 cf. the fate of the pre-Islamic gods and spirits in Arabia, Koran *Sura* XXXVII. For general indications of the universality of such syncretisms in Islam, see Gibb,1947, pp.23ff.; Milliot, 1949, p.643.
21 See Massignon, Encyclopaedia of Islam, IV, p.668.
22 Among the Christian and Muslim (Cushitic) Agao of Gondar, this syncretism leads to the co-existance of figures like Zaar Abba Yusuf (Christian) and Zaar Sheikh Mahammad (Muslim); Leiris, 1934, (1), pp.126-9.

Chapter 2

SAINTS IN THE LOCAL PRACTISE OF ISLAM

THE QAADIRIYA DRUMMED *DHIKRI*

In this chapter we move decisively out of the library, where I began my Somali studies, into the 'field' where, like every anthropologist, I relied for information primarily on direct observation and questioning. Based in what was then the Somaliland Protectorate, in 1955-7 I divided my time between visiting pastoralists (mainly the Dulbahante of Las Anod District) and northern agro-pastoralists (the Jibril Abokor), living to the west of Hargeisa, where they combine traditional animal husbandry with the cultivation of sorghum. While working in the latter region, I used to stay in a small settlement, called Oodejiid, near the Ethiopian border. It was there, through the good offices of local sheikhs I had come to know, that I was able to attend the weekly 'remembrance' service (*dhikri;* Ar. *zikr*) held on Tuesday evenings in honour of the Qaadiriya founder, Sayyid 'Abdul Qaadir Jiilani, in the local 'bush' Koranic school. At a typical service on 4 July, 1956, my field notes record that by about eight in the evening, some sixty men (including youths) were crowded together in this small school shed, where the teacher slept at night and taught during the day.

The proceedings were directed by three sheikhs, sitting on a mat in one corner and grouped round an incense burner which also provided heat. At the other end of the room, six kettles filled with tea were hissing on a small fire. Sheikh Muuse Sh. 'Abdullahi led the rites, reading the saint's birthday service (*mawliid*) from a manuscript Somali copy of the printed Arabic version. The *dhikri* opened with the singing of a praise song (*qasida*) for 'Abdul Qaadir written by a Somali sheikh, Yusuf Bakr (of the Sheikhaash priestly lineage). As with the saint's *munaqib*, this was chanted by the three presiding sheikhs, the rest of the audience joining in the refrain, accompanied at regular intervals by bursts of drumming. The drums were beaten vigorously by pairs of young students of the Koranic school, each armed with two small drum sticks. There was keen competition for this role and, as one pair became tired, they were immediately replaced by another.

With the liberal distribution of perfume, the atmosphere created by the recitation of the praises of the saints, the chanting, and the drumming struck me as particularly warm and harmonious. It was impossible also not to notice the rapt, trance-like attention on many faces. The warm-hearted feelings which participants evidently experienced were extended to include me – despite being a non-Muslim outsider, and in other contexts apt to be labelled, like other non-Muslim foreigners, a *gaal* (strictly 'infidel').

The hymns in Arabic, fully understood only by the sheikhs, contained a plenitude of mystical sentiments, appealing to the saint to 'bathe his adherents in his love' while the lay participants recorded how their saint's 'love' and the 'love of his people' stirred the heart. Each pause in the chanting of the praises was marked by each person present reciting the *fataha*. The expression of this boundless love for the saint by people not readily given to sentimentality in their arduous daily lives, was explicitly linked by them to the sounds of the music and drumming. The love of your soul, I was told, is awakened and quickened by the drumming. The drummers themselves seek God's blessing (Allah-*bari*), they told me, when they drum and thus benefit directly from the saint's blessing (*baraka*).

While at this weekly service, food is restricted to the tea refreshments liberally distributed, the annual celebration of Al-Jiilani's birthday is marked by a more elaborate and prolonged ritual (using the same texts), which includes feasting on livestock as well as chewing the stimulant leaves of the *qat* plant (see Lewis, 1961, p.222).

The other principal events in the local religious calendar are not specific to adherants of the Qaadiriya *tariiqa*, but shared by everyone whatever Order they follow. These are the pan-Islamic *iid al-fitr*, marking the end of the Ramadan fasting month (known in Somali literally as 'hunger'), and a time for almsgiving in grain to sheikhs and the poor; the *iid al-arafa*, celebrating the time of pilgrimage to Mecca when sheep are killed for a large local congregation; and the Prophet's *mawliid* (birthday). In addition to these major international rites, here as elsewhere in Somaliland, people generally celebrate the birthday of Sheikh Yuusuf al-Kawnayn (see Ch. 7), some making the pilgrimage to his shrine at Dogor – where three visits are considered equivalent to going once on pilgrimage to Mecca itself.

The other saints venerated locally, usually once each year, are the

founders of proximate lineage ancestors and the clan-family eponym, Sheikh Isaaq, whose remembrance day (*siyaaro*) is usually held
after the grain has been harvested. Not many people, however, are
able to make the long and arduous journey to Sheikh Isaaq's actual
tomb at Mait on the Erigavo coast and have to resort, consequently,
to venerating him at a local memorial site, *maqaam* (literally a place of
visitation), where his spirit can be contacted. In this rural area, there
is more emphasis on these saints' days than on the Friday prayers,
since as local people say, there are no suitable large buildings able to
accommodate enough worshippers.

The Qaadiriya Order generally might perhaps be characterised as
the most accommodating of the *tariiqas* to local customary Somali
practise: for example, not requiring women to be veiled, accepting
and adapting *qat*-chewing as an aid to staying awake during the
night-long religious vigils, and permitting (but not always utilising)
a drum music accompaniment. More significantly, in terms of the
appropriateness of Sufism to Somali institutions, the emphasis
placed by the Qaadiriya on the cult of saints readily encourages the
sanctification of Somali lineage ancestors. Most of those men (for
women are rarely directly involved) who attend Qaadiriya ceremonies are not formal initiates (*muriids*), and being largely illiterate in
Arabic have no direct access to the written corpus of works celebrating its founders and their rich mystical lives which B.W. Andrzejewski (1974), and more recently B.G. Martin (1992) and S.S. Samatar
(1992), have explored in detail. But, as indicated in my account of the
Oodejiid drum *dhikri*, lay participants may lack sophisticated knowledge of Islamic mysticism, yet manifestly enjoy similar rhapsodic
experiences to those described so elaborately by the religious leaders
themselves.

THE SIGNIFICANCE OF ATTACHMENT TO AN ORDER

The most esoteric aspects of Islamic mysticism are pursued inside
the religious communities (*jama'as*) which, as noted in Chapter 1,
have been established in areas suitable for cultivation. In the 1950s
there were over a dozen of these (mainly Qaadiriya) in Somaliland
and a total of over eighty in Somalia. Of these over half were Ahmadiya, and the remainder distributed almost equally between Qaadiriya and Saalihiya[1]. The much larger number of settlements in the
south, of course, reflects the more promising agricultural conditions
there, especially between the rivers in Digil-Mirifle territory, where
some operated successfully as banana cooperatives. As well as being
propagated in such sedentary religious communities (with

populations ranging between a few score and several thousand), the teachings of the Orders are also disseminated by itinerant sheikhs and their followers (known as *hir*) who move amongst the pastoralists, following the latter's grazing movements in the different seasons. It is in such mobile religious schools[2] particularly, that camel-boys and young male herders generally, may acquire the rudiments of Koranic instuction and some familiarity with the Arabic litany. Here, as in traditional sedentary Koranic schools (such as that at Oodejiid, above), they learn to write passages from the Koran on thin, leaf-shaped wooden black-boards (*looh*), using ink made from charcoal and resin.

Without being formally members of particular Orders, and although some people belong to more than one, in towns the majority of the laiety attend mosques which belong to a particular Order. It is not surprising, therefore, that the potential rivalry between Orders and their followers (which cross-cuts lineage adherance) is expressed in religious processions, and not infrequently flares up into physical conflict. Such hostility was, of course, especially marked during the Saalihiya jihad led by Sheikh Mahammad 'Abdille Hassan between 1900 and 1920 (see, above, p. 12), a party of whose supporters assassinated the famous Qaadiriya leader Sheikh 'Uways at Bioley in 1909. Sheikh 'Uways, who was a prolific author of learned mystical treatises as well as of fiery polemics against Mahammad 'Abdille Hassan and his 'Dervishes' (as they called themselves), is now venerated as probably the most important saint in southern Somalia (S.S. Samatar, 1992, pp.12, 25).

In line with his own caustic attacks on the cult of 'dead' saints, so far as I know, Mahammad 'Abdille Hassan is nowhere regarded as a saint (although his followers certainly venerated their founder, Sayyid Mahammad Salih, as a saint). While Mahammad 'Abdille Hassan's *jihad* cast the Saalihiya Order in Somalia in militant opposition to the Christian colonisers of his country (Ethiopia, Britain and Italy in particular), the assumption that the Qaadiriya remained, in contrast, acquiescent and even collaborated with the colonisers, has been shown to be misinformed by B.G. Martin's careful historical research. Using a wealth of sources, largely untapped before by western scholars, Martin (1969; 1976) has explored the political role of the Uwaysiya branch of the Qaadiriya. It becomes apparent that, through his close personal links with the Zanzibari rulers, Sheikh 'Uways promoted resistance to the European colonisers in German occupied Tanganyika, and even Uganda and the eastern Congo.

The other main branch of the Qaadiriya amongst the Somali is the Zayla'iya, named after the famous Somali ecstatic mystic, Sheikh

'Abdirahman Ahmad az-Zayla'i (also known to Somalis as the 'the Radiant', *nuuriye*) who died in 1882, and was largely responsible for speading, or embedding the Qaadiriya in the north. It is interesting to note that, despite basing his operations at Qolonqol in the Ogaden, and apparently being named after the historical northern Somali town of Zeila (but see Martin, 1992, p. 13), like Sheikh Uways (who was a Tunni Torre from Brava) this charismatic pioneer traced his roots to humble, ex-slave, origins amongst the Digil Mirifle.

Thus, both the pillars of the Qaadiriya in nineteenth century Somalia came from southern ex-slave families and, as Islamic leaders in, respectively, the north and south, cut across this territorial (and to some extent cultural) division. In the south, the Saalihiya in their turn, as we have seen (above, p. 12) were also led by a sheikh of ex-slave origin. The fiery northern Somali Saalihiya leader Mahammad 'Abdille Hassan was, in contrast, of northern pastoralist Ogaadeen-clan origin, but in the context in which he launched his *jihad* amongst the Dulbahante of Somaliland, he was also to a significant extent an outsider (albeit an affine).

As we have seen, the Saalihiya had no monopoly of anti-colonial resistance. In addition to the external activities of Sheikh 'Uways in the south, the Qaadiriya in the north strongly opposed attempts by the British administration to open secular schools (misrepresented as Christian missionising)[3]. On the other hand, although the Saalihiya, as a branch of the reformist Ahmadiya, had historic links with the Wahhabis, the small Dandaraawiya[4] *tariiqa* – which was more closely Wahhabi in derivation and orientation – opposed Mahammad 'Abdille Hassan's movement. This hostility no doubt reflected the Isaaqi identity of the Somali Dandaraawiya sheikhs but was also in line with the pro-British stance of the founder himself, Sayyid Mahammad Dandaraawi who died in 1908.

THE POWER OF SAINTS

Like the Dandaraawiya, the Saalihiya are more puritanical than the Qaadiriya. Both the former Orders encouraged the veiling of women, especially in towns and settlements, banned the stimulant drug *qat* as well as tobacco, and sought to apply the Shariah more strictly than was generally the case in Somali society where it was strongly modified by the influence of Somali customary law (*heer*).[5] The principle theological division between the Saalihiya and the Qaadiriya Orders in Somalia, however, concerned the power attributed in Sufism to saints and their intercessory role (*tawasul*). The Qaadiriya maintained the traditional Sufi belief that the blessed

powers (*baraka*) bestowed *post mortem* on saints offered an effica-
cious means of access to the Prophet and the bounty of God. The
Saalihiya officially maintained that only living saints – such as during his lifetime, their founder, Sayyid Mahammad Salih – possessed
this grace. However, in practise, Mahammad 'Abdille Hassan himself composed a famous religious poem praising Mahammad Salih
for his saintly virtues, and the founder was certainly so regarded
after his mortal life was over.

ATTITUDES TOWARDS SAINTS

The term we are here translating as 'saint' is the Somalised Arabic
weli (*pl. awliya*). While in Arabic this translation is controversial since
the literal meaning of the Arabic word is 'friend' (of God), in Somali,
as B.W. Andrzejewski (1974, p.35) has emphasised, the term is used
exclusively to mean a saint, capable of performing miraculous deeds
(*karamat*) through the blessing (*baraka*) which God has given him.
There is a vast corpus of Somali oral and written (hagiographical)
Arabic testimony to the remarkable powers of saints. While the performance of many, probably most of these miracles are general to
the genus saint, others are specific to particular saints. Routinely,
saints foretell the future, see events at a distance and miraculously
intervene in them, recover lost objects, heal the sick (and dispense
mystically charged prophylactics), bring rain, and secure fertility
and general prosperity – Aw Barkhadle (below, Ch. 7) is an outstanding example. They also appear in dreams and at times of personal difficulty and crisis.

These are all of course attributes of positive charisma. There are
corresponding hints that their miraculous powers may be employed
less benevolently, against enemies for example, and this understanding informs the general belief that it is potentially dangerous to
injure them or their property. The descendants of Sheikh Muumin
(see below, Ch.6), living in the rich arable lands of southern Somalia,
specialise in mystical crop protection, a specialisation matched in
similar farming regions elsewhere. So, for example, this is also the
primary role of Sheikh Ibrahim Lanshone at Gebile in the north-
west whose son (in the 1950s) received homage (*siyaaro*) to protect
the growing crop. In common with a number of others and justifying his protective power, this saint was particularly famous for his
skills in communicating with birds and animals.

Typical examples of miscellaneous miracles reported to have been
performed by a medley of local saints in the north-west are the following. Sheikh 'Osman Sheikh Nuur, a leading Qaadiriya sheikh in

Somaliland in the 1940s and 1950s, by praying to God successfully arrested a serious flood in Burao town when the local seasonal river (*tug*) overflowed disastrously. On another occasion, a herdsman who was looking after his camels stole a beast from another group (a common activity of young herdsmen) and brought it with the sheikh's herd to water at the wells in Burao. The sheikh noticed the stolen camel and ordered that it should be returned to its owner. But the herder refused to do this. The sheikh then prayed that the looted camel should be separated from his herd. When the camels had finished watering and were being mustered to leave the wells, the stolen camel sat down and refused to budge. Its owner turned up a little later and claimed his missing camel which, of course, the sheikh gave him with many apologies.

In another case, a follower of this saint was arrested by the Ethiopian authorities and ill-treated in prison. In his distress he turned to the sheikh and composed a praise poem (*qasida*) extolling his virtues. The door of the prisoner's cell miraculously opened and would not close however hard his captors tried. Eventually, puzzled and frightened by these mysterious developments, his captors released the prisoner. On another occasion, when the saint was dictating some of his *qasidas* to a pupil late at night, the lamp suddenly went out. The saint raised one of the fingers of his right hand, and light shone out like a beacon enabling the edifying work to continue.

Another saint was seen to turn into a lion in a mosque and, at another time, to have been seen in Mecca (by a prominent Somali politician – Mahamad Haji Ibrahim Egal) when he was actually in Burao. This sheikh had a disobedient son who went mad and was put in the lunatic asylum at Berbera. However, the saint prayed for his recovery and he was restored to his senses and became a sheikh in his turn.

In keeping with his great fame, many remarkable miracles are attributed to Sheikh 'Abdirahman Zayla'i. It is related that twelve sheikhs came from the ancient Islamic centre of Harar and asked him for a copy of a learned book. Unfortunately, the sheikh only possessed a single copy, but he asked one of his assistants to bring the book from his library and place it inside a box. The sheikh then recited prayers over the box and the next morning instructed his assistant to look inside where he would find a number of copies. 'Take one copy for each of the twelve sheikhs, two for yourself, and one for me', he instructed. Each copy was inscribed with the words, 'In the name of Sheikh 'Abdarahman az-Zayla'i'.

In the same bookish spirit, it is also recalled that Sheikh 'Abdarahman Zayla'i possessed a large gelded camel which carried his portable library from place to place as well as water vessels for his ablutions before prayers. This mobile library camel was immune from attack by wild animals. However, on one occasion, the camel went astray and was found by some wicked herdsmen. They wanted to slaughter the animal, but some of the party protested that this famous camel belonged to the sheikh and should not be killed. One herdsman nevertheless insisted on his plan although he could not persuade his colleagues to assist him. He struck wildly at the camel's neck with his spear, and the spear sprang back dealing him a mortal blow while also killing the camel. His companions were astonished and dug a grave in which they proceeded to bury him. As they lowered the body into the grave, the grave refused to accept the corpse and spewed it up. They tried again with the same result. After seven attempts, astonished and exhausted, they gave up and set off to find the sheikh to confess to him what they had done and to ask his pardon. Sheikh 'Abdarahman responded: 'I forgive you; eat the camel's meat [which they had left untouched]. I have forgiven the man who killed my camel and the grave will now receive him.' So, at last, they buried the robber who had dared to molest the sheikh's property.

This account, like the previous one, is culled from a collection of stories about the saint's life and miracles. It was inspired in an unusual but appropriate way as B.G. Martin (1992, p.13) reports: A Qaadiriya brother from Brava drempt on Saturday night, 17 January 1952, that the saint had appeared to him, proposing that the record of his divine graces (manaqib) should be collected and recited every year at the memorial service at his tomb on the anniversary of his death (1882). The person who had this dream entrusted the task of compilation to several other sheikhs who eventually collected eighty-four hagiographical manaqibs 'drawn from the learned and mouths of men and from loving brothers of the tariiqa'. The results were published in Cairo in 1954.

Like his colleague, Sheikh 'Uways was also a man 'full of wonders' as B.W. Andrzejewski (1974, p.20) puts it, translating an oral text he collected in northern Kenya. Once about 700 of his students who were very hungry came to the Sheikh saying: 'We are hungry, what can we eat?'. 'If God decrees it, tonight you will eat abundantly', replied Sheikh Uways. When the sun set, the sheikh came upon a huge swarm of flies which had settled on the ground for the night. He then prayed: 'My people are very hungry. I want these flies turned into sheep and goats for me!' And God turned the flies into sheep and goats. Half were slaughtered that night.

In another story collected and translated by Andrzejewski (1964 p.142), a man who had lost his livestock was advised to visit Sheikh 'Uways's tomb at Bioley in southern Somalia and told that when he got there he should weep and ask God's help – this would ensure the return of his animals. The man followed this advice and slept beside the tomb. At midnight, one of the sheikh's disciples appeared to him as he slept and spoke to him. The herdsman woke up and when the disciple asked him what had happened, he said, 'Some time ago I lost many animals – sheep, goats, and cattle – and I searched for them but could not find them. Now I have come to ask the sheikh for help, and on my way to his tomb I prayed for assistance as I walked along.' 'The sheikh says to you,' said the disciple, 'that you should now go to sleep. When dawn comes, the animals you lost will come to the tomb, and then you can drive them home.' So the herdsman went to sleep, and when dawn came, to his great joy he saw the animals. Then he slaughtered two head of cattle in gratitude and as an offering in honour of the sheikh.

SCEPTICISM ABOUT MYSTICAL POWERS.

While, as the foregoing suggests, a very considerable oral Somali literature as well as texts in Arabic (some published) testifies to and indeed magnifies the mystical efficacy of saints as wonder-workers, attitudes towards them are often ambivalent and tinged with scepticism. Indeed, popular Somali culture where these records of saintly miracles are enshrined, is also rich in accounts of false holymen and fraudulent saints who prey upon the credulity of the unsophisticated. This is often associated with references to the generally grasping greed frequently attributed to holymen. Such commentaries on the venality of the pious are regularly encoded in proverbs. So, according to one common saying: 'If you pluck a louse from a holyman in the dry season, he will think you intend to give him something'. The moral here being: avoid holymen in case they demand alms.

There is in fact a wide range of such 'counter-hagiographies', or 'anti-legends', as B.W. Andrzejewski (1974), who presents a good selection of the genre, calls them. Tales abound, for example, of would-be holymen concealing torches (before these objects became commonplace) under their clothes to give the bearer the impression of being bathed in mystical radiance. Others recount how sheikhs, claiming to offer mystical fertility to barren women, practised a rather direct form of therapy. Other accounts of prophetic predictions are revealed to be contrary to the actual run of events, and claims to heal the sick and terminally ill are likewise exposed as mischievous tricks taking advantage of those desperately in need of help.

Sometimes a rational, secular explanation is proposed for seemingly miraculous events. Thus someone I knew quite well, and who had little Western education, told me the following didactic tale: A herdsman in the interior recounted his baneful experiences during a drought in which, day after depressing day, he had seen his livestock die of thirst. Himself driven desperate by lack of food and water, one night as he was mournfully contemplating his plight, an ancestor appeared before him in a dream with the reassuring message that he should be of good cheer as rain and prosperity were on the way. The next day, rain did indeed fall, and grass quickly sprang up (as it does after drought) to feed his few remaining head of livestock. These in turn recovered their strength and soon began to increase – prosperity was returning. Jubilant at his good fortune, the herdsman built a little shrine to his ancestor at this place and offered a thanksgiving sacrifice. He soon broadcast these miraculous events to his clansmen, calling attention to their ancestor's provident intervention. Following this, his clansmen organised an annual memorial service (*siyaaro*) in honour of the ancestor, and those who attended over the years often reflected on the benefits conferred on them by their generous ancestor who repaid their attentions so liberally. This was the official hagiography.

However, according to my iconoclastic friend, the truth was very different. What had actually happened was that the herdsman who initiated this ancestor cult had, in fact, cynically buried some pigs' teeth in the ground at the 'sacred' spot. Hence, the sense of well-being and prosperity felt by the clansmen who paid their ancestor cult at this (unholy) place had nothing whatsoever to do with intrinsic mystical power. They were simply experiencing the Durkheimian pleasure of socialising together and transforming social intercourse into religious transcendence.

To get a more rounded picture of the context of scepticism, I should add that the person who offered this profoundly sociological analysis of the Somali ancestor cult also told me that reports of American and Russian space exploration current in the 1960s were completely false. They were simply super-power propaganda, for the Islamic cosmology taught that there were seven vaults in Heaven which man could not penetrate. Other Somalis reacted in the same disbelieving way to such radio reports of space exploration (cf. Helander, 1998).

FUNDAMENTALISM

While the increasing impact of Western secular education and the media since the late 1940s and early 1950s has, obviously, reinforced sceptical attitudes towards the powers claimed for saints, similar critical currents have long been present in local Somali Islam itself. Sufism is after all a long contested tendency in mainstream Islam, and certainly from the nineteenth century, if not before, 'fundamentalist' trends have attacked the cult of saints, being powerfully reinforced by Wahhabi influence from Arabia.

Within his campaigning Saalihiya, Mahammad 'Abdille Hassan, as we have seen, strongly denounced the traditional cult of local (ancestor and other) and international saints – while treating Mahammad Salih, the living founder of the eponymous Order, as though he were a saint. But he was by no means alone in this, nor the first to do so. A slightly earlier, and probably theologically more influential figure, was Sheikh 'Ali 'Abdarahman 'Majerteyn', born in 1845 in Nugal, who travelled as far as India in search of wisdom. After sojourning in Mecca, he returned to Las Anod and thence visited Mogadishu, eventually settling in Merca, where his shrine is a place of pilgrimage (he died in 1913). Sheikh 'Ali (or Haji 'Ali, as he is sometimes called) was a learned sheikh and is reported to have written at least thirteen books in Arabic. Preaching doctrines which were close to those of the Wahhabis, he attacked saint 'worship', pilgrimage to saints' shrines, music, smoking and all sensual excesses. He condemned all the regular *tariiqa* rituals, *dhikri, hadra,* and *shellaad.* One of his books (written in Somali-Arabic) records his learned exchanges with Qaadiriya leaders at Qolonqol settlement (founded by Sheikh 'Abdarahman Zayla'i). Ironically, contrary to his own teaching (and unlike Mahammad 'Abdille Hassan), he is popularly regarded as a saint. This line of criticism of 'vulgar Islam' as virtually heretical was continued into the 1960s by a learned northern Somali sheikh, Sheikh Nuruddiin 'Ali, who published a swingeing and closely argued polemic in favour of what Andrzejewski (1974, p.36), in a comprehensive and sympathetic summary of the work, calls 'Islamic monotheism'. He was not, of course, alone in this.

Under 'Scientific Socialism' and the oppressive rule of General Mahammad Siyad Barre in the 1970s and 1980s, Islam provided a potential vehicle for opposition to the regime[6]. These cicumstances encouraged the search for alternative Muslim principles as a basis for political organisation[7], a quest which became increasingly pressing, if difficult to achieve, in the chaos that followed the collapse of the Somali state in 1991.

With the disappearance of the national legal system and police force (both already in decline under Siyad's arbitrary rule), traditional Somali customary law (*heer*) re-emerged to provide a network of compensation arrangements for delicts which operated in the old decentralised fashion alongside spreading violence and the shifting power of fickle war-lords.[8] These unstable conditions naturally favoured movements, on the part of some leaders – often supported by traders and merchants – to set up Shariah courts, administering a 'fundamentalist' law of talion on the Saudi Arabian model. Such courts were most effective when their operation was supported by a dedicated Islamic militia. And just as these same conditions, with the abundant supply of modern weapons, favoured the rise to prominence of military big men or war-lords, with their personal and clan-based militias, so sheikhs claiming a reformist mission were also encouraged to establish similarly equipped (and often competing) centres of power. To facilitate the supply of external support, in money and weapons, from friendly Arab states, local leaders of all sorts found it expedient to play the Islamic card. This largely became the militarised pattern of the 'new' fundamentalism of the 1990s with armed groups such as the *Wahhabi Al-Itihad al-Islam* competing for control of local resources with traditional clan groups and their militias. Some hostile Somali critics claimed that far from being made up of religious zealots, 'ninety-nine per cent of the young men who form[ed] part of this organisation hardly knew more about it than its name'.[9]

This bellicose movement, which at various times has announced that its objective is to reconstitute Somalia as a Shariah-based state, was involved in serious armed conflict with local clan militias at Kismayu, Merca and Mogadishu and, in 1992, unsuccessfully sought to wrest control of the thriving north-eastern port of Bosaso from the local Majerteen-based Somali Salvation Democratic Front militia. Following this resounding defeat, in which the self-styled *Muhajadiin* lost many lives, the *Itixaad* (Itihaad) regrouped in Gedo region, in Marrehaan territory up the Juba river, where they soon became embroiled with the Marrehaan SNF militia. With the backing of supporters in Saudia Arabia and other Arab countries, the organisation was able to recruit paid followers and to subvert local attempts (which had UN and other international support) to establish a regional administration in Gedo. The Marrehaan traditional leaders, as well as the SNF, complained to the *Itixaad* leadership about their destructive local impact, charging them with subjecting local people to starvation at a time when there was plenty of food and resources in Somalia.[10]

In the mid-1990s, this 'religious' organisation became involved in guerrilla actions against agents of the Ethiopian government in the Ogaden (Region Five) across the Somalia border, as well as allegedly in terrorist attacks in Addis Ababa itself. This provoked a vigorous Ethiopian response which included air-strikes at the *Itixaad* base at Lugh on the Juba river. These retaliations by Somalia's 'traditional' Christian adversary, were considered in some quarters to justify the unfolding jihad which this group of fundamentalists claimed to be waging.

While the *Itihaad's* high profile military activities have tended to eclipse other less ambitious fundamentalist movements, they have also tended to throw into the shadow another tendency on the part of the traditional Sufi Orders to regroup under their own reformist banner. Here the principal jihad is that of the individual's soul, the cultivation of which is fully compatible with strict adherance to the Shariah. The fact that in these bitter times in Somalia the ideally distinct holymen (*wadaads*) have taken to arms like the traditionally opposed category of lay warriors (*waranleh*), puts the onus of the distinction on the religious, whose specialist knowledge, and practise of the faith becomes increasingly important if they are to maintain their traditional role and distinctiveness.[11]

Notes

1   Figures taken from AFIS records.
2   Interestingly, the same pattern of nomadic schools was followed in the Mass Literacy Campaign of 1975: see Lewis,1988.
3   The most serious incident involved a riot at Burao in 1921, in which a British District Commissioner was killed, when the administration attempted to open a school at this important centre.
4   See Lewis, 1961,p 220.
5   See Lewis, 1961.
6   See Lewis, 1988.
7   Two organisations, in particular, *Ahli* and *Wahdadda*, strongly influenced by Saudi and Egyptian sheikhs whose message reached Somalia in books and on cassettes, developed in this period. See Aqli Ahmed, 1986.
8   See Lewis, 1993a; 1993b; 1994; 1995; 1996; 1998. Helander, 1997; 1998.
9   Idaajaa, 1995.
10   See Idaajaa, op. cit.p.13.
11   See below, Ch. 4.

Chapter 3

THE LEGITIMACY OF WRITING

THE ORAL LEGACY

Separated as they are by only a narrow strip of sea from the centre of Islam on the Arabian peninsula, the Somalis have for over a thousand years participated at least in some degree in this universalistic literate culture. They have, however, reacted to this long exposure to Islam in ways which, as I have argued in chapter 1, are broadly consistent with their own traditional structure and culture. Thus, amongst the northern nomads a popular form of Sufism laying stress on the veneration of saints, which fits nicely with the traditional lineage structure and cult of ancestors, is strongly developed. The Sufi brotherhoods are also well represented amongst the southern cultivating Somali. But here, where lineage ties vie with territorial connections in importance, agnatic ancestors figure less prominently, and less automatically, as saintly mediators between man and God. In both regions, until very recently, the most notable achievements of local literate culture have been those produced within this Sufistic tradition. Despite their long Islamic history, however, as far as is at present known most of this local religious literature is of comparatively recent origin; and little seems to have been produced, or if produced, to have survived from before the nineteenth century. Such Arabic manuscripts and a few published works written by Somali sheikhs usually take the form of hagiologies, although there are also some legal works, Koranic commentaries, and treatises on etiquette and Arabic grammar (see Appendix II).

This apparent dearth of any strong corpus of locally written literature reflects the fact that only a small portion of religious men are in fact fully literate in Arabic. In general, knowledge of reading Arabic is more widely diffused than full literacy, competence in which has until recently been the monopoly of a small religious elite. In this

generally uncentralized traditional society, the role of men of religion enjoying various degrees of literacy has in any case been rather
narrowly circumscribed. Basically, these sheikhs or, as they are also
known locally, *wadaads*, are expected to act as mediators between
man and man and between man and God. They do not normally
hold political office and in the first capacity their competence is traditionally restricted to peace-making and arbitration, to the recommendations of Shariah awards of compensation for injuries and
death, the administration of Muslim principles of inheritance (in certain cases), the solemnisation of marriage, divorce, and all other matrimonial matters. In the second they are regarded as ritual officiates
possessing the appropriate liturgical lore for the conduct of all religious occasions, the treatment of sickness and misfortune with
Koranic remedies, and are similarly relied on as astrologers, divin-
ers, soothsayers, etc. As we shall see presently, many of these traditional functions have been formalized and institutionalized in the
colonial and post-colonial periods.

Men of God thus play essentially mediating roles and, in the
absence in Somali history – at least since the sixteenth century – of stable, large-scale centralized Islamic states, have not acquired a wider
range of positions of authority: nor has literacy in Arabic traditionally
overflowed much outside their ranks, despite the connection
between trade and Islam. For, although a considerable proportion of
these sheikhs have functioned as teachers, sometimes with peripa-
tetic students wandering around the Somali bush and largely
dependent on charity, they have not brought general literacy to the
laity. The exigencies of the nomadic life allows few nomads to attend
such schools regularly or over long periods, and teaching is in any
case for the most part limited to learning the Koran by heart and not
directed towards teaching writing as such. Traditionally then, the literacy rate of men is very low, and for women almost non-existent.

Another factor which seems of significance in contributing to the
surprisingly slight extension of literate Arabic culture notwithstand-
ing the Somalis' long exposure to Islam, is the high development of
oral communication. The Somali language is a particularly rich and
versatile medium and its speakers are very conscious of its literary
resources, which, it might be added, are closely geared to the circumstances of their society. Just as, for example, the society is highly
acephalous and democratic, so the language is highly egalitarian: it
is very difficult to express honorific titles in Somali, for almost none
exist traditionally. At the same time skill in rhetoric and poetry is
highly prized (Andrzejewski and Lewis 1964). Thus it is no accident
that the majority of the most outstandingly successful leaders have

been men who have won wide acclaim in these fields and whose poetry is often still remembered (e.g. Sheikh Mahammad 'Abdille Hassan[1]). More directly, Somalis appear to regard oral communication not merely as a refined art, but as a basic essential for successful survival. This may sound trite, but I wish to emphasize that there is an explicit and articulate evaluation of the importance of oral Somali which in one significant context can be illustrated by the following encounter. In an entirely spontaneous manner an illiterate nomad was once explaining to me the advantage of learning foreign languages, and more particularly of speaking the language of the country you happened to be in. If you did not speak the local language, he observed, how could you possibly know what people were saying about you? How could you know what their intentions towards you were? They might be plotting to kill you, and you would not have the defence of prior warning. This evaluation of oral communication is of course here directly related to the overwhelming Somali assumption that, unless there is very strong evidence to the contrary, the world is essentially hostile.

With this accent on the necessity for mutual intelligibility, oral Somali is used, particularly in the form of poetry, as an extremely important medium of mass communication. The power of the tongue and of the spoken word in spreading hostility and enmity, in countering it, or in broadcasting conciliatory messages, in ruining reputations or praising men to the skies, is very evident in Somali culture. Rapid and highly effective oral communication, and for that matter not merely the dissemination of news and gossip, but also of cultural innovations, is, I think, facilitated by the strongly nomadic bias of Somali society. Despite the low density of the population, pastoral movements most effectively spread news and information whether it is encapsulated in memorable verse or merely relayed in prose. Each meeting of nomads functions as a relay station for the onward transmission of messages.

In fact the oral tradition is so strongly developed and so highly prized that, as we have noted, there is a certain, mainly religious, oral treasury of poetry in Arabic as well as in Somali. But, of course, this is a two-way process. And although there is no record of when the process first occurred, the Arabic script has long been used as a medium for Somali as well as Arabic – or for a mixture of both. Various suitably modified scripts, better adapted to the special needs of Somali, have been developed locally as well as several quite independent non-Arabic scripts of which the phonetically most sophisticated and widely known is that called Osmaniya after its inventor, Osman Yusuf Kenadid (Lewis 1958). This alphabet and script, some of whose characters resemble Amharic, was invented about 1920 and initially enjoyed a limited currency amongst its inventor's close kinsmen and friends. Later on, in mid-century, and benefitting from an association with the contemporary spirit of modern Somali nationalism, its usage spread for a while.

THE IMPACT OF LITERACY

If one of the factors which seems traditionally to have hampered the spread of literacy in Arabic is the richness of the indigenous oral culture and its close adaptation to a predominantly nomadic setting, this is not to say that writing has had no significant impact in Somali society. In what follows I shall examine salient aspects of Somali social structure which do seem to me to have been affected by this literate presence. Although it is not always easy in the nature of the case, to make the separation between Islam the religion and Arabic the language that it happens to be so closely associated with, I shall try to indicate those effects which appear to depend upon writing as a factor rather than simply to inhere in Islam as such.

Let us begin by considering the range of dispute-settlement procedures. Here the first thing to note is that all Somalis, irrespective of their lineage affiliation, recognize a common morality and common procedures for the settlement of disputes. This is in fact one element which defines the boundaries of the Somali nation. Thus, although traditionally they were not united in a single political unit capable of acting concertedly, they did acknowledge uniform categories of wrong, and they possessed common means of settlement and restitution through the exchange of damages according to a common tariff. This tariff is based upon the law books of the Shafi' school of Islamic Law and is applied in specific cases by literate sheikhs. Its details are in general so complicated, providing for the operation of so many contingent factors, that I do not think such a corpus of damages could be effectively maintained except in writing. Prior to colonization, such rulings on the amount of damages appropriate to a particular injury provided a basis for negotiations in disputes between lineages where arbitrators were called in. There was no formal machinery for enforcing such awards except that engendered by the desire of the parties to a dispute to make peace, and this, of course, was a function of their relative strengths and of the total political situation at any point in time. Ultimately, force or its threat was the final sanction supporting a settlement. In the colonial and post-colonial situation these awards became judgements enforceable by an official hierarchy of courts operating with the full support of the state.

Before the collapse of the Somali Republic, the procedure was as follows. The nature of an injury was first established by a doctor and then referred to a Kadi's court where the corresponding damages are assessed. A plea for payment was then filed in a court which might reduce the actual amount if it considered it unrealistically large or inconsistent with Somali custom. Similarly, even in cases of homicide, when the murderer is caught and sentenced, claims could be preferred for damages, particularly if the sentence awarded was light. And when, as frequently happened because of lack of evidence, a conviction was not obtained, a suit for blood-compensation would be filed and often successfully sustained. This, it should be added, applied even today in the case of traffic accidents in towns.

Here, then, we see the use of literacy as an important element facilitating dispute settlement on a national basis. This is equally evident in a parallel set of procedures which overlap with those just described. Here I refer to the fact that every Somali is by birth or choice the member of a particular compensation-paying group which provides for the security of his life and property. These insurance associations are basically composed of agnatic kin whose diffuse kinship obligations are given specific definition and content by a contractual treaty which stipulates the terms of their common indebtedness. Such treaties state the amount of damages appropriate to particular categories of tort occurring within the group, and also lay down the proportions in which outgoing damages received from other groups will be disbursed internally. Such treaties mirror the structure of the group to which they refer. And the actual amounts of compensation for injuries, which are usually set at a lower rate within the group than that obtaining between groups, are again ultimately derived from the Shariah law books of the written tradition. I hasten to add, however, that Islamic law here receives a peculiar Somali interpretation which is in fact contrary to the letter and spirit of the law. For while Shafi' law considers the culprit in deliberate homicide to be primarily responsible for making restitution without the support of his kin, Somalis regard the contractually defined kin group to be collectively involved, whatever the circumstances of a killing. Their practice thus runs counter to the Shariah, and their awareness of this is one of the components of the tension which exists in Somali culture between Islamic and customary morality, a point I shall return to later. This is another aspect of the existence of written tradition here regarded as a standard and immutable repository of ideal conduct.

Yet writing affects the position more fundamentally than this. These treaties, based on consensual agreement normally amongst agnates, have since colonial times been recorded in writing, whether in Arabic, English or Italian. Thus recorded, they are lodged in the local District Office of the area regularly frequented by the groups concerned. Every District headquarters maintains (or did so up to 1990) a register of these '*dia*-paying' (from the Arabic *dia*, blood-money) group agreements, which have come to be accepted as defining the political and legal status of the individual members of the group concerned. They are consequently now a source of law, since their existence is taken to define the legal status of any individual who is involved in a dispute. These, of course, are not immutable or unchanging documents anymore than the placement of particular groups and the overall balance of power in the Somali segmentary system are fixed for all time. Thus, as groups change their segmentary alignment and unite or divide according to the context of disputes and as they see their interests, individual treaties are modified, abrogated, or rescinded and new ones submitted to the local representatives of the centralized government – now universally regarded as the final arbiter in disputes.

Although there is some indication that prior to colonization such treaties were sworn at the tombs of important saints and thus authenticated and solemnized, I find it difficult to be certain that such procedures could effectively uphold the validity of these treaties in the way and to the extent provided by the presence of a neutral third party – namely centralized (colonial) government. But whatever may have been the situation in the past, what now seems clear is that the practice of recording these *dia*-paying group treaties in writing and lodging them with the government has had the effect of giving greater definition and rigidity to these units than they seem to have possessed in the past. If the level of agnatic grouping most frequently stabilized or 'frozen' in this way is, in any case, that order of segmentary grouping which most effectively answers the adaptive needs of the total Somali setting, its distinctiveness has nevertheless been increased in relation to other potential levels of association. Amongst the northern nomads where the *dia*-paying group thus defined is a low-level lineage, some five to eight generations in depth with a maximum population strength of a few thousand, this seems to have had the effect of reducing solidarity at wider and higher levels of grouping. Thus, there is some indication that those much larger lineage groupings which because of their size (up to 100,000 strong) I call 'clans' had, in the past, greater rigidity as social units than they do today.

However, the primacy of social factors here and the true character of the complicated interplay between them and the use of written records are suggested by the contrasting situation amongst the southern cultivating Somali, who provide a convenient control in analysis. Here the comparable solidarity groups representing the main axes of politico-legal action and affiliation, and possessing written treaties defining their unity, are in fact very large clans up to a population size of 100,000. This contrast, as I argue below (Ch. 5), corresponds to the expansion of political solidarity in the south associated with the occupation of stable arable territories and the widespread adoption of clients. Thus, I am suggesting that in both cases writing here has further stabilized levels of group association which basically correspond to different adaptive needs.[2]

WRITING AND GENEALOGIES

This discussion leads directly to a consideration of the influence, if any, of writing on the form and content of Somali genealogies. A marked feature of this society is the very long genealogies, sometimes consisting of more than thirty named ancestors, which are regularly and widely known. As in other segmentary lineage systems, these genealogies which children are taught to memorise at an early age are primarily concerned with establishing the identity of individuals and groups. Thus Somalis are fond of comparing this system of placing a person rather loosely with the use of street numbers and house addresses in Europe. Of course, among the Somalis, genealogical classification carries immediate political and legal implications which are not normally conveyed by European addresses. When strangers meet, the normal procedure is for them to ask each other their pedigrees and for these to be traced until a point of reference which is mutually significant is reached. This can be done in two ways. One can ask a person's name and then that of his father and further ancestors until a significant referent is reached; or one can begin at the top and work down, simply asking the question: 'Of what group are you?', over and over again until the relevant point is reached. The relevant point varies to some extent with the circumstances, but it is unnecessary to go into that here. What is important is that the question 'Who are you?' is answered in genealogical terms and behaviour is, broadly speaking, adjusted accordingly.

The importance of this system of placement even in the modern urban setting can be gauged from the fact that when a few years ago it became fashionable to pretend that 'tribalism' had been replaced by the strength of nationalist fervour, one asked not a person's lineage, but his 'ex-lineage'. And indeed the English affix *ex-* became adopted into the Somali language so that one could perfectly acceptably ask someone his 'ex-', when one could not directly ask his lineage affiliation. More recently, this ingenious sophistry has been discarded in a climate of opinion which increasingly accepts that lineage divisions and hostility persist and cannot thus be suppressed but must simply be accepted as a basic, if unpalatable, fact of life. With this background and given the fluidity of Somali political groupings, the question which of course at once arises is: are these genealogies mere charters mirroring current political commitments and alignments and changing when they change? In the first place, the answer to this question depends upon whether one is concerned with the northern nomadic Somali or the southern cultivators.

Amongst the nomads one finds within the same lineage segments of very unequal strength and correspondingly disproportionate genealogies. Telescoping and foreshortening certainly seem to occur in what are known locally as 'short branch' lineage genealogies. But 'long-branch' genealogies appear to conserve what is broadly a relatively true record of successive ancestors up to the level of clans, or those wider lineages that because of their extreme size I call 'clan-families'. Amongst the southern Somali, genealogies have a much more uniform character; they are generally much shorter and there are not usually such wide discrepancies between collateral segments. Here there is abundant evidence of genealogical manipulation and distortion, indeed all of those processes which, as amongst the Nuer and Tiv and elsewhere, maintain a close correspondence between the genealogical model and actual structural relations. These differences can be referred to the fact that among the southern cultivators the adoption and full genealogical assimilation of clients is a constant and regularly recurring process. In fact, the southern clans are vast federations composed of persons of every possible genealogical origin. Among the nomads, in contrast, adoption and genealogical client assimilation are rare. With them the constant process of political alliance and realignment is validated by the explicit contractual treaties we have discussed, rather than by genealogical manipulation. There are in practice two ideologies or models, the genealogical and the contractual; and in general the genealogical idiom provides the guidelines for action rather than defining or circumscribing this completely. Now this is also true of the southern cultivators, but the range and effectiveness of these two ideologies differ between the two groups. The political units of the cultivators are larger, less fluid and fleeting, and ultimately stabilized by land interests. Contract, broadly speaking, operates significantly only at an inter-clan level. Amongst the nomads it operates at all levels, as occasion requires, and is a more pervasive instrument of group definition. Thus for the southerners there is a wider social range of interaction, where relationships are defined genealogically rather than by contract, and genealogies are more subject to manipulative processes. In each case, consequently, the situation is that where social relations are ultimately defined by contractual treaties rather than by agnation alone, genealogies are less open to adjustment.

How is all this related, if at all, to writing? If northern genealogies are less distorted than southern pedigrees it might be supposed that the northerners are more literate. This, however, is not the case: indeed, if anything, the reverse is true. Moreover, the genealogies of which I am speaking are seldom in fact conserved in writing. Lineage genealogical lore is part of the oral tradition, taught, conserved and transmitted mainly by word of mouth. I say 'mainly' because there is one area of genealogical lore which does tend to be conserved in writing. This is typically that part of the genealogies which reaches outside Somali society and postulates Arabian connections validating the Somali profession of Islam (Lewis 1994, Ch. 4). In fact, standard Arabic genealogical handbooks have a certain limited circulation and knowledge of them is by no means rare amongst literate sheikhs. Moreover, the local hagiologies which celebrate clan and clan-family ancestors as saints of power and pedigree invariably contain appropriately exalted genealogies tracing connection to the family of the Prophet Mahammad. Although they state historical truths in the manner of a parable, these genealogies which are written are probably the most spurious of all.[3]

This evidence seems fully in accord with the situation in other societies with a specialized and restricted literate tradition and written genealogies, such as the Chinese.[4] It suggests that with only a limited currency, writing in a society which does not abound in disinterested, disengaged positions which might promote genuine historicism does not necessarily serve to preserve the literal truth. In this culture where it is traditionally associated with holy writ and has magical significance, writing appropriately enough serves to validate the genealogical charter of the total society, and in this sense helps to conserve its genealogical shape at the highest levels of agnation.

RIVAL LITERACIES

In the Somali case, the examples we have considered serve to show how the influence of the slender literate strand has been heavily affected by the structure of the traditional illiterate society. This seems consistent with what might be called the lubricatory role of its main bearers, sheikhs and men of religion, oiling the wheels of social intercourse, rather than throwing spanners in the works. Yet, the situation is not as simple or as clear-cut as this. For the existence of an unchanging written corpus of Islamic morality to which constant reference and appeal are made, and which is regarded as the final source of truth and the ultimate guide to human conduct, means that actual behaviour as well as popular morality is constantly open to scrutiny in a way which would not obtain in the absence of writing. As in other societies there are, of course, double standards and several layers of morally charged ideologies. Put at its simplest, there is the Islamic model of conduct as set forth in the Koran and law books; there is the popular morality, Somali 'custom', of which Somalis have a very explicit awareness; and, finally, there is actual practice. These are all interrelated, and ultimately the last two, according to local views, are referable to the first for their legitimacy.

Somalis are generally aware of those major respects in which their practice and customary assumptions part company with Islamic ideals. In certain important areas of life, as for example in the frequency of fighting and feud and its resolution according to uncanonical compensation arrangements, there is an explicit tension between the Islamic model and the local model and practice. In traditional settings this has tended to provide pressures towards modernity in the sense of the growth of national solidarity and the suppression of lineage enmities and hostilities. Today, however, the Islamic ideal world-view stands in a somewhat ambivalent relation to modern social change. Here it is necessary to recall that although the Muslim cosmology emphasizes an eschatological doctrine which contrasts sharply with the closed traditions of tribal worlds, it also encompasses many aspects which are regarded as archaic and impractical in most modern Islamic states. Thus while, on the one hand, some passages in the Koran can be used to provide ammunition for a modern view of monogamy which is increasingly popular amongst the young Western-educated Somali elite, other elements oppose new ideas and social change, at least among the least sophisticated. So, as we have seen (Ch. 2), when news of rival Russian and American space-flights was broadcast in Somalia, some traditionalists claimed that this was nothing but Communist and anti-Communist propaganda. The Koran, it was said, revealed clearly that there were seven heavens and man could never penetrate these.

Thus, in effect, one literate tradition is now increasingly challenged by another and attempts to reconcile the two are only partially successful. At the same time, independently of this, the mass of the Somali population have been, as it were, jerked into the modern world of mass radio communication and pop songs very largely through the medium of their own unwritten language. Again, new items of a foreign literate tradition are being selectively adapted to traditional needs and interests, at the same time contributing towards overall social change. And in the post-colonial scramble for education and literacy by all age-groups, and both sexes, despite their traditional religious affiliation, English is tending to emerge as the preferred written language, thrusting Arabic and Italian into second place. Since the widespread adoption of the official written Somali script (using the Roman alphabet) in the mid-1970s, this has become the main rival to written English. For Somalis, it has the great attraction of preserving many of the crucial features of oral Somali and is best seen as an 'extension in writing of oral culture in which there was already a tendency towards fixed forms'(Lewis, 1986, p.148).

Notes

1   Sheikh Mahammad led the Somali nationalist insurrection from 1900-1920 which was designed to free his people from alien Christian rule. His brilliant success as a leader was closely connected with his consumate powers as a poet. He made extensive use of poetry as a political weapon in campaigning for support against his enemies.

2   In this context the probable stabilizing effect of writing seems supported by the contrasting situation among the Baggara nomads, where each payment of compensation evokes a different pattern of solidarity and compensation-paying arrangements do not appear to be recorded in writing. See Cunnison (1966).

3   These remarks, of course, do not apply to those specialized religious genealogies by which office-holders and prominent sheikhs in the religious orders record the names of their teachers and their celebrated predecessors in the spiritual hierarchy. These 'chains of blessing' (*silsilad al-baraka*), as they are called, are almost invariably written and act as, in effect, diplomas of religious instruction and illumination. Such professional *tariiqa* pedigrees are an important source for the local history of the orders in Somalia.

4   See Freedman 1958 and 1966. In this context Bohannan's assumption that illiteracy is a precondition for genealogical manipulation and that this could not be sustained in a literate society seems to me naive (Lewis, 1961).

Chapter 4

SACRED AND PROFANE IN SOMALI SOCIETY[1]

THE SUFI TRADITION

The theocratic sentiments of traditional Islam concede no clear-cut division between spiritual and secular authority. Yet, on the whole, it is probably only in the first centuries of the Muslim era that the religious and secular powers of the state have been completely fused. Nevertheless, despite the gap between Muslim political ideas and Muslim governmental practice, the ideal of theocratic rule still retains much of its force in Islam. And in all Muslim countries even today, when there is generally a widening gulf between traditional Islam and modern secularism, there is still a strong tendency for the division between spiritual and secular affairs to be effaced or at least partly bridged in certain contexts (cf. Milliot, 1949; Fakhry, 1954). This is as true of the Somali situation as of other Muslim nations and applies in both traditional and modern social contexts. In this paper I discuss some aspects of this problem, but by no means all,[2] in terms of the distinction which Somali make between 'men of religion' (*wadaaddo*, sing. *wadaad*) and 'warriors' (*waranleh*, lit. 'spear-bearer'), the widest and most basic occupational division which they traditionally recognize.

As will presently be shown, there are in fact several categories and several grades within the general classification 'men of religion'. But for the moment it will suffice to note that while the term *wadaad* refers to a man of God as distinct from a warrior, Somali also employ the Arabic title 'sheikh' synonymously, usually, however, reserving it for those *wadaads* whose religious education and knowledge is above the ordinary. Thus the expression *wadaad* refers both to a general category of persons ranked 'men of God', and, more specifically, to those religious experts less well-versed in the Koran and Shariah, and less literate in Arabic, than those for whom the title sheikh is reserved.

Sufism and saint veneration – the most characteristic features of Somali Islam – seem, as I have suggested in chapter 1, particularly well-adapted to the Somali segmentary lineage system. Certainly Sufism which lays such stress on the powers of intercession of saints has readily accommodated local Somali lineage cults and practices. Thus, as we have seen, a large proportion of those saints who now occupy a prominent place in Somali Islam are in fact the ancestors of local lineages. Not all the saints venerated by the Somali, however, belong to this category. Of those who are not revered as the ancestors of local lineages, the most outstanding are the founders of the Sufi Orders or 'brotherhoods' (tariiqas) which Somali follow.[3] Those with the greatest following are the Qaadiriya, and the Ahmadiya and its various branches. The former is the oldest and best-known Order in Islam, founded by Sayyid 'Abdul Qaadir al-Jiilani, who died in 1166; the latter was established by the noted reformer Sayyid Ahmad ibn Idris al-Fasi who died at Mecca in 1837. Although the Qaadiriya may have existed locally in some form considerably earlier[4], northern Somali today (at least in the ex-Protectorate) place the local development of the tariiqas in the nineteenth century.

Today, as in the Muslim Near East in the eighteenth century (Gibb and Bowen, 1957, p. 76), attachment to these Orders is practically synonymous with the profession of the faith and almost all Somali follow a tariiqa. The Somali approach to the Prophet and worship of God is almost exclusively channelled through Sayyid 'Abdul Qaadir or through Sayyid Ahmad. The Orders know no lineage boundaries, and Somali of different and often hostile clans and lineages worship God through the same 'brotherhood'. Attachment is to a particular Order to which their ancestors adhered – unless they are subject to missionary influence from a new Order. And here it is necessary to emphasize that for the majority of the Somali, attachment to a particular tariiqa is merely nominal and means little more than that those who support the Order attend the religious services conducted by sheikhs of that Order (cf. Ch. 2).

The official organisation of the orders is hierarchical, particularly so among the Ahmadiya, who are strongly bound to their headquarters at Mecca where their local leaders ultimately derive their authority. The Qaadiriya, on the other hand, has no effective ties with Baghdad, its historical centre, and the authority of its sheikhs is defined locally by previous local leaders according to their charisma and works and local Somali following. Thus, among the Qaadiriya, there are generally more sheikhs who claim to have 'authority' to administer the rites of the tariiqa to novices and to campaign for converts, than among the Ahmadiya whose official organisation is more centralised. In each, those sheikhs who hold authority to transmit the *tariiqa* are known as 'sheikhs of *tariiqa*' and such *tariiqa* leaders are found in all the principal administrative centres and towns where they attend to the affairs of their adherents. Subordinate to these regional leaders are a number of *wadaads* and sheikhs who have been fully initiated into the rites of the Order by their superiors. These are followed in the religious hierarchy by novices (sing. *muriid*) who are still under instruction and who are often grouped in itinerant theological schools about their sheikh and teacher. Finally there is the vast mass of the Somali population who are warriors (*waranleh*) and in no sense *wadaads* and for whom the *tariiqa* which they support is little more than a vehicle for the profession of Islam. Thus, *wadaads* and warriors alike follow a particular Order and many *wadaads* and sheikhs hold a position of authority in the *tariiqas*. But there remain a considerable number of sheikhs and *wadaads* who, though they support a particular Order, have no official position in it, and whose religious status depends on their knowledge, learning, and works, quite independently of their adherence to an Order.

Both Orders aim at the full achievement of the ideal of Muslim brotherhood independently of the clan or lineage affiliation of their adherents. This ideal is most closely approached in the self-contained religious settlements (*jama'as*) consisting of men of different lineages living together as brethren (*ikhwan*) under their sheikh. Such distinct theocratic social units are rare in northern Somaliland although there are a considerable number in the arable areas of the south. Thus for the northern Somali who make up the majority of the population, adherence to a *tariiqa* does not represent a renunciation of lineage ties or of the pastoral life, but merely a common bond of religious interest which ideally at least is opposed to sectional rivalries.

Although the Qaadiriya and Ahmadiya share the common aim of furthering Islam through their services, and for the young through innumerable Koranic schools, they are divided by considerable doctrinal differences. Fundamentally these turn on the respective religious powers of their founders. Through his godliness and virtue the founder of an Order is held to be near God, or even to have achieved identification with the Creator, and to exemplify in his teaching the true path of devotion. His blessing falls on those who follow his teaching and example and celebrate his ritual offices.

This esoteric conflict is reflected in external differences between the two Orders. The Ahmadiya are as a whole more puritanical than their rivals and prohibit smoking and the chewing of the stimulant leaves of the *qat* plant [L.*catha edulis*), activities which the Qaadiriya do not frown upon and even consider proper to religion occasions. Again, as we have seen, the Qaadiriya weekly services (*dhikri*, lit. 'remembrance') held on Tuesdays and Thursdays are more flamboyant, and usually begin with a hymn-singing procession to the mosque or other place of worship, while the Ahmadiya rites held on Sundays and Wednesdays lack this feature and are generally more restrained. In keeping with these differences in the larger towns each Order usually has its own mosque. These features reflect the rivalry which characterizes the operations of the Orders despite their avowed common purpose, and sometimes give rise to bitter hostility and even physical conflict completely contrary to their ideals.

WARRIORS AND MEN OF GOD

The power of the *tariiqas* depends upon the extent to which individual worshippers feel themselves to be far removed from the virtue and glory of God. For Somali are well aware that the endemic wars and feuds which divide their society are contrary to the teachings of the Prophet and his condemnation of bloodshed within the Muslim community. The very distinction which Somali draw between warriors and 'men of God' expresses the dichotomy they see between their pastoral warring life and the ideals of Islam. Thus men turn for aid to the saints and seek the help of *wadaads* and sheikhs to bless and pray for them.

Wadaads (using this term to refer to all men of religion irrespective of their precise religious status) are, as we have seen, men who have acquired knowledge of Arabic and the Koran and Shariah and other devotional books and who, whatever their primary means of livelihood, are in some sense devoted to religion. Many in fact depend primarily upon the same resources as warriors; many own herds of camels and flocks of sheep and goats and live as pastoral nomads, or in the cultivating areas as cultivators; others earn their livelihood in the towns as merchants and traders and use their religious knowledge only as a subsidiary source of income. Few are completely engaged in religious activities and entirely dependent on charity for their subsistence.

Any man who through his religious knowledge comes to be regarded as a *wadaad* and is given the title 'Aw' before his name, (or, if his knowledge is greater, is styled sheikh), irrespective of his mode of livelihood, is regarded as a 'man of God' and not a warrior, and is expected to fulfil his religious roles that are not given to warriors.

Wadaads attend to the religious affairs of their lineage or local community, and if there is a mosque and a sufficient congregation, direct the Friday prayer as well as the Sufi services. In addition to officiating at all religious ceremonies and the Muslim calendrical feasts, they solemnise marriage, advise on the interpretation of the Shariah in divorce, and to a limited extent in inheritance.[5] Most importantly, in a society regularly harried by strife, they assess compensation for injuries according to the Shariah law books. They also sell amulets and prophylactic potions, bless the sick in prayer and sacrifice, and similarly treat livestock diseases. When a well or water-hole is being excavated, or some other similar collective enterprise is undertaken, characteristically they do not participate directly but limit their exertions to exhortations to the workers and prayers for their success. In the towns their role in marriage, in the apportionment of estates, and the assessment for compensation of physical injuries, is formalized by their appointment as government stipended Kadis, i.e. as Muslim magistrates with authority mainly in matters of personal status.

In contrast to the position in some other Muslim tribal communities, in Somalia *wadaads* are not primarily political leaders, and indeed are by the very nature of their calling theoretically excluded from full participation in secular politics. In lineage councils, especially those concerned with political issues and fighting, *wadaads* are expected to bless the words and decisions of the elders who make policy, but not to participate in policy-making. In the case of the most humble *wadaads*, however – those whose knowledge of religion is slight – it is often difficult to make a strict separation between spiritual and secular functions, since many of these take their place on lineage councils as elders despite the fact that in other contexts they act as *wadaads*. But the more learned and more important sheikhs do not participate in lineage policy-making in the same way that warrior elders do. Their role is ancillary and concerned with securing the blessing of God on the enterprise of their kinsmen, and not officially, at least, in deciding the nature of these enterprises.

In keeping with this, men of religion are highly valued as go-betweens and as members of peace embassies because they are by definition non-combatants and ideally stand above particularistic loyalties. But although they often take these duties seriously and were encouraged to do so by the colonial administrations, they are not entitled to decide the rights or wrongs of an issue. This is a matter for a panel of arbitrators, and the political decision involved in accepting or rejecting a settlement lies with the elders of the parties concerned, not with the sheikhs. Thus, although, as mentioned, they assess damages for physical injury and bloodshed, they take no part in the process by which their awards are claimed or obtained. This is the concern of secular lineage courts, and ultimately if all else fails, settled by force. The furthest sheikhs can go in mediating is to bind hostile parties by an oath against further violence, and such oaths in practice do not deter men from fighting when the pressures which lead to hostilities are acute.

For all these and other services, men of religion are rewarded with presents rather than by payment. A few indeed depend wholly on charity for their livelihood. For, although Somali sometimes regard wadaads as a class as grasping, they generally treat men of religion generously. Despite the fact that many are wealthy, wadaads are grouped as an ideal category with the poor and needy and those who for one reason or another are weak in secular power – all these enjoying the special protection and blessing of God. Any kindness shown to them pleases God and brings an automatic reward, if not in this world certainly in heaven. These attitudes towards wadaads are consistent with the division which Somali ideally see between secular and religious affairs and power, and this, as will be seen presently, leads to other properties which are assigned to wadaads but not to warriors. Here it may be noticed that some of the most powerful and important sheikhs come in fact from small lineages whose political status is weak.[6]

MYSTICAL POWERS

Thus, wadaads who are by definition ideally neutral in lineage affairs, if not always in practice so, mediate between man and man and between man and God. This applies to all wadaads, irrespective of whether or not they hold offices in an Order. And because of their calling they are expected to adhere more strictly to the precepts of Islam than are the warriors who, as has been said, are aware of their failings and look to their sheikhs and saints for support and intercession. In general, wadaads are more regular in their prayers and fasting and will not readily eat meat from stolen livestock although warriors show little compunction in this. Indeed, sheikhs claim that they will not even join with warriors in the feast of an animal which has been seized from a kinsman as a legitimate punishment for an infringement of dia-paying solidarity.

With their non-participation in fighting, and ideally at least disengagement from secular politics, wadaads enjoy a measure of ritual protection which warriors lack. As we have seen in chapter 2, it is both shameful and dangerous to attack the property or person of a man of God and instances are cited, especially by sheikhs, of the misfortunes which have befallen those who failed to observe this rule. Sometimes a sheikh is employed to curse the footprints of an unknown thief in the belief that this will cause illness and ill-luck to dog the miscreant until he returns the stolen goods. In practice, although the ideal sanctity of men of religion is not fully honoured, sheikhs nevertheless enjoy a measure of security from wanton attack by warriors. Here to a considerable degree the ritual sanctions which are held to protect *wadaads* vary in their effectiveness with the religious status of the person concerned. To take a typical example, when after severe fighting two northern Somali clans were concluding peace, settling outstanding blood-debts, and returning looted stock, camels which in the heat of battle had been seized from the herds of a leading sheikh of one side were returned with greater alacrity than those belonging to his warrior clansmen.

Thus, to men of religion mystical powers are attributed which warriors do not possess. Ultimately warriors rely on force in settling their disputes, and political status is defined in terms of fighting strength. Since sheikhs are by definition non-combatants and ideally may not resolve their differences by an appeal to physical force, it is not surprising that warriors should credit them with employing mystical means not only to protect their persons but even to advance their personal aims and ambitions. One interpretation widely held by warriors of the long drawn-out illness of a government Chief Kadi was that he had been cursed by rival sheikhs who coveted his office. I have never heard such insinuations advanced in strife between warriors. And indeed though magic, sorcery and witchcraft play a small part in northern Somali life generally, warriors believe firmly in the mystical powers of sheikhs, although they do not always respect these powers in conflict between lineages.

Yet despite the ideal disengagement of men of God from fighting, and partly because the majority of the supporters of the Orders are warriors and not *wadaads*, conflict between the *tariiqas* sometimes leads to violence. During the rebellion against Christian rule in northern Somaliland between 1900 and 1920 led by Sayyid Mahammad 'Abdille Hassan (the so-called 'Mad Mullah') rivalry between the Saalihiya Order (a branch of the Ahmadiya) which he supported and the older established Qaadiriya assumed an acute form. In general the Qaadiriya sided with the administration against the Dervishes, as they were called, and each *tariiqa* abused the other in sermon and hymn, one celebrated Qaadiriya hymn going so far as to proclaim that 'to kill one of these (the Dervishes) is better than to kill a hundred infidels'. This antagonism eventually led to the

assassination by a party of Mahammad 'Abdille's forces of one of the
most famous Qaadiriya sheikhs, Sheikh 'Uways. (see Ch. 2)

The struggle between the Qaadiriya and Saalihiya still continues,
especially in northern Somaliland where in the late 1950s in the
north-east the Qaadiriya took the offensive, seeking converts in
areas where the Saalihiya were established. In this campaign it
appears that the infiltrating Qaadiriya have sought to play off lineage and clan jealousies to their advantage in an effort to extend their
sphere of influence. Incidents have been numerous. In 1955 a clash
occurred between congregations of the two Orders at Ainabo, a
watering place in the northern Haud. The Qaadiriya in the town had
staged a religious procession and were marching toward their
mosque singing hymns in praise of their founder Sayyid 'Abdal Qaadir. On their way, they stopped provocatively outside the Saalihiya
mosque and a fight quickly developed which was stopped by police
intervention with the arrest of thirteen people. Three of these were
wadaads of the Saalihiya and the remaining ten members of several
different and often hostile clans, of the Qaadiriya. This incident,
which illustrates the transcendent character of *tariiqa* affiliation in
relation to clanship, also shows how, despite their condemnation of
violence, men of religion are sometimes driven to forsake their ideals and to resort to the tactics of warriors in their conflicts.

Such factionalism between the Orders, however, while indicating
their role in cutting across clan and lineage boundaries should not be
taken as evidence that clanship is normally subordinate to religious
affiliation. For in the much more common wars and feuds between
lineages these *tariiqa* clashes are regarded as minor scuffles, and
when warriors are divided by hostility between their lineages such
common religious affiliation as they may possess is of little moment.

Moreover, it is not merely that *wadaads* are sometimes driven to
behave like warriors in religious disputes, for ultimately like warriors *wadaads* also depend upon the support of their clansmen for their
security in this warring society. Religious charisma alone is not a sufficient protection. And to this extent the ideal division between men
of God and warriors, and between spiritual and secular affairs
breaks down. Many sheikhs, it is true, attack in their sermons and
preaching the traditional system of *dia*-paying responsibility[7] and
roundly condemn bloodshed within the Muslim community. But
when all is said and done, few can afford to disregard those ties and
responsibilities towards their kin which in this militant society represent their ultimate safety. Although they officially denounce the
collective payment of blood-wealth which helps to perpetuate strife
and minimizes the responsibility of the individual, most sheikhs are

still a party to the *dia*-paying agreements of their clansmen. It is with these rather than with God that the security of their property and person ultimately lies. Thus, however unwillingly, men of God are almost inevitably drawn into the secular political system.

The overwhelming influence of the pastoral social system in drawing men of religion into its orbit and weakening the theoretical distinction between warriors and *wadaads* is seen, especially in northern Somaliland, in the existence of a number of priestly lineages. These are regarded as *wadaads* as distinct from warriors although they have the same economy, social organisation, and political structure as warrior clans and lineages and like the latter are divided into *dia*-paying groups. Varying in individual strength between a few thousand and twenty or thirty thousand, these religious lineages are known collectively as *Reer Aw* (from 'Aw' the title prefixed to a *wadaad*'s name) or simply as *wadaaddo* (pl. of *wadaad*). There are two main classes. There are first priestly lineages which trace their charisma and descent from an immigrant Arabian saint and therefore stand outside the Somali genealogical system; secondly, there are those whose saintly ancestors are local Somali and who accordingly stand side by side with warrior lineages within Somali clans. Those of both groups are in effect minor Sufi Orders, organized in the form of lineages, although their members also profess adherence to one of the main *tariiqas* (i.e. to the Qaadiriya or Ahmadiya). The marriage of religious and secular organization which they represent is clearly seen in their genealogies. Every religious order in Islam preserves its 'chain of blessing' (*silsilad al-baraka*) – the list of those saints through whom, from the founder to the present head, the Order has been transmitted – and opposes this to the secular genealogies of its affiliates, in these Somali religious lineages the two genealogies are fused. Their genealogies which unfold from their lineage ancestor and religious founder are at once their 'chain of blessing' in a religious sense, and also the mainspring of their political solidarity in a secular sense.

It might be thought that by this criterion all Somali lineages – those which include both warriors and *wadaads* and those with only the latter as members (i.e. *Reer Aw*) – are in effect religious Orders. For most warrior lineages and clans, certainly the larger groups, regard and venerate their ancestors as Sufi saints. There remains, however, a clear distinction – at least ideally – between the two types of lineage in terms of the distinction which Somali make between warriors and men of God. However unlearned and ill-equipped in formal religious knowledge they may be, all the members of a priestly lineage are regarded by definition as *wadaads*. In contrast, in warrior lineages, only those are regarded as men of God who have acquired religious knowledge: here the status of *wadaad* is attained individually by achievement and not transmitted by birth.

Although, however, all the members of priestly lineages are regarded as men of God by definition, not all in fact practice as such. And, as has been indicated, they participate in the warring pastoral social system. Yet because they nevertheless retain the collective status of *wadaads* they are considered to possess blessing, and retain a mystical power which warriors lack. This, like individual sheikhs in warrior clans, gives them a measure of protection from wanton attack and enables them to act as mediators in disputes. Hence, although these religious groups are in organization and structure indistinguishable from warriors and sometimes act as though they were warriors, they yet retain their special religious position, just as *wadaads* in the national *tariiqas* conserve their ritual status although they sometimes also behave as warriors. Thus the involvement to varying degrees of men of God in secular politics does not necessarily completely vitiate their special religious qualities.

RELIGION AND PRACTICAL POLITICS

These priestly lineages illustrate, I think, the overwhelming influence of the arid ecological conditions of northern Somalia and of the accompanying pastoral social system. For the independent self-contained *tariiqa* settlements in which *wadaads* are able to place themselves outside the prevailing social and political conditions are extremely rare in the north, though not uncommon in the fertile regions of the south. Outside the few such communities which have attained an autonomous politico-religious status, sheikhs are inevitably caught up in the workings of the pastoral political system. A few outstanding religious leaders, however, are said to have taken oaths binding themselves not to be a party to *dia*-paying group payments. And in the towns, where collective security is not at such a premium as it is in the interior of the country (at least in the period 1950-90), some sheikhs have aligned themselves with the nationalist political parties in espousing the cause of national unity, calling for an end to partisan strife (cf. Lewis, 1958). Here it seems that modern nationalist politics offer a field of activity in which the conflict between religious and secular authority is minimized.

This is not altogether without precedent in the past. Before the rise of modern nationalism, the men of God have sometimes been able to achieve positions of at once religious and political leadership in national issues involving opposition between the Somali people as Muslims and the Christian administrations. Perhaps the best example is the case of Sayyid Mahammad 'Abdille Hassan's rebellion referred to above. (See Jardine, 1923; Caroselli, 1931; *Encyclopaedia of Islam*, vol. iii, pp. 667-8.) 'Ina 'Abdille Hassan', as he is familiarly remembered by Somali, began his campaign as a zealous reformer and fervent proselytiser for Mahammad Salih and his *tariiqa*. Early contact with Christian missions and disagreement with the administration of what was then British Somaliland, however, soon led him to launch a holy war against the missions and against all those who acquiesced in Christian rule. This jihad, which was conducted with remarkable success over a period of twenty years, has its analogies in the Sudan Mahdiate and other similar Muslim movements. By an appeal not only to charisma as a Muslim leader but also with the aid of every traditional Somali tie which he could cultivate, the Sheikh created a loose but extremely effective military organization operating from various bases in northern Somalia. His rule was theocratic but much more informally organized and fluid than that of the Sudan Mahdi.

The movement itself, which some modern nationalists regard as anticipating their own struggle for national unity and independence, illustrates better perhaps than any other example how despite the theoretical division between religious and secular power, particularly in a national Muslim context, sheikhs can emerge as political leaders. Here the position is not so much that men of God have been caught up in the web of clan politics because of their agnatic loyalties and interests, but rather that they have used these devices to create a politico-religious organization on a national front based upon the aim of Muslim unity. Secular political power has been acquired by men of religion in a national Muslim context, as was also the case in the 1950s and 1960s with those sheikhs who were leaders of national political parties (see also contemporary 1990s movements, above p. 44).

❑

In the foregoing I have examined some of the social implications of the division which contrary to the theocratic spirit of Islam Somali ideally draw between religious and secular affairs. Preceding from the premise that the spheres of interest and authority of men of God are different and distinct from those of warriors, who form the majority of the population, Somali regard each as having access to different types of power. Ideally the power of warriors is restricted to secular affairs and in the last analysis depends upon the use of physical force and upon numerical strength ('penis count' as Somalis put it); that of men of religion is based on the power of God.

Yet, as in other societies, for the most part men of God have to live in the secular world and find themselves involved in its values and practices. In Somalia, with the partial exception of those living in self-contained religious communities, this secular involvement is clearly defined in terms of common livestock interests with warrior clansmen and common (warrior) *dia*-paying obligations. This engagement in the secular system weakens the rigidity of the ideal cleavage between religious and secular occupations and between spiritual and worldly power. At the same time, the practical force of the division is also reduced by the secular power which sheikhs can acquire in national issues when the appeal to common loyalty is based partly upon the ideal of religious identity. Yet despite this, men of God retain religious power and authority which warriors lack; a situation which to Somali is no more confusing or inconsistent than the divergence between religious ideals and worldly reality found in most human societies.

That the ideal division between the two spheres often breaks down in actuality is of course in keeping with the theocratic temper of Islam; and indeed with the very nature of Islam as a religion which seeks to regulate the affairs of its adherents in all departments of life. But this is not something which is peculiar to the Muslim Somali or to Islam itself, for it seems rather to proceed from the very nature of power and its relation to social organization. Power in general is not readily defined in a single cultural idiom, or divided into separate secular and spiritual spheres any more than those whose social roles are primarily defined in either of these two spheres can entirely limit their interests to that realm alone. And in Somali society the vital social interests which warriors and men of religion share, and particularly those which make *wadaads* dependent on warriors for their ultimate safety, prevent any rigidly comprehensive and permanent division between the two spheres.

Notes

1   This chapter is primarily based upon field-work carried out in Somaliland between 1955 and 1957 and financed by the Colonial Social Science Research Council, London.

2   I have not the space here to discuss the part played by Islam in the constitution and governmental organization of the independent Somali state.

3   As we shall see in later chapters, there are also a number of important saints of immigrant origin who appear to have had no particular

connection with the Orders and who came to the country many centuries ago to convert Somali to Islam.

4 See Trimmingham, 1952, p. 240.

5 Generally, in the interior of northern Somaliland, Somali ignore the provisions of the Shariah in respect of the rights of female heirs. This is especially true in regard to such major livestock as camels. In the towns, however, fuller authority is often given to the Shariah and women more often inherit property than they do in the interior.

6 Compare Montagne, 1947; Evans-Pritchard, 1949; J. Carlo Baroja, 1955; and *Encyclopaedia of Islam*, vol. iv, article 'Shaikh', p.275.

7 According to the Shafi'ite School of Islamic Law, which most of the Somali follow, a person who commits intentional homicide is alone responsible for making reparation and should not be supported by his kin as he is here.

Chapter 5

THE LIE OF THE LAND IN SOMALI ISLAM

In discussion of social change in Africa it is often forgotten that some of the most pervasive and sociologically arresting examples of cultural adoption and adaptation have occurred under the impact of Islam. Like other world religions, and perhaps more than most, Islam indeed offers a particularly rich field – so far quite inadequately exploited – for the systematic study of the way in which different social systems and cultures react to a common external stimulus. This field of research is all the more important, since it offers a unique opportunity for confirming and enhancing the synchronic sociological analysis of traditional institutions. For if traditional institutions have the forms and functions attributed to them by sociologists it must be possible to explain, at least in part, the patterns of assimilation which arise with the adoption of Islam. There must be some logical correspondence between the traditional structure of a society and the manner in which it interprets Islam. Here, surely, is an interesting field for comparative sociological analysis.

With this in view, in this paper I seek to show how within the broadly integral Muslim culture area of the Somali of north-east Africa salient differences in traditional social organization are reflected in correspondingly different patterns of Islamic assimilation. The variations in this common culture area on which I wish to focus attention are those which distinguish the pattern of life and social system of the northern nomadic Somali from their southern and part-cultivating kinsmen. These differences are accompanied by and, as I shall argue, intimately connected with corresponding variations in Muslim religious organization.

THE GEOGRAPHICAL AND HISTORICAL SETTING

In the relatively barren environment of the nomadic pastoral Somali the husbandry of camels, sheep, goats, and sometimes cattle, is the dominant pattern of life, with cultivation restricted to a few areas of high rainfall, mainly in the north-west. Within this overwhelmingly pastoral world, with its characteristic nomadic ethos, the southern Sab Somali, consisting of two main clan confederacies (the Digil and the Rahanwiin), occupy the wedge of relatively rich arable land between the Shebelle and the Juba Rivers in the south of the Republic. Although the Sab still practice animal husbandry extensively, their main interests lie in their fields, where they grow sorghum and a variety of other crops. Unlike the pastoralists, they occupy stable village settlements set in the centre of their arable lands.

This difference in economy and way of life, keenly felt by both groups, is accompanied by a variety of cultural differences, of which the most immediately striking is the possession by the Sab of a separate and quite distinct dialect which differs from the speech of the northern Somali to much the same extent as Spanish does from Portuguese. And in the genealogical idiom in which social relationships are phrased throughout the Somali culture area, this division between the northern nomads and southern cultivators, as we have seen, is reflected in the national Somali pedigree where each division is traced to a separate founding ancestor.

These distinguishing features and others to be noted presently are the outcome of distinctive historical processes in the two regions. Over the last thousand years or so the Somali people as a whole have been engaged in a large-scale, but uncoordinated movement of expansion from the north. In the course of this tide of migration, in which clans and lineages, often in conflict, jostled each other forward, a wide variety of groups settled in the arable lands between the Shabelle and the Juba and mingled there with other ethnic groups, particularly with parties of Oromo and north-east coastal Bantu. Out of this amalgam – which is restricted to this area – the Sab clans emerged with their distinctive characteristics and with a sense of separate identity within Somali culture as a whole, which is matched by the northern nomads' traditional contempt for cultivation. This process is well reflected in the derivation 'large crowd' popularly given to the Sab clan-name 'Rahanwiin'.

Both these areas appear to have been exposed to Islamic influence for a similar period, for both the northern and southern Somali coasts have unquestionably been in extensive contact with the Muslim world for almost a thousand years. The ancient trading stations, developed, if not founded, by Arab and Persian Muslims about the tenth century, along both coastlines are a testimony to this. Moreover, from the little that is at present known from the history of Muslim contact, there appears to have been no salient difference in either the source or nature of Islamic penetration between north and south. Certainly, today all the Somali are Sunnis of the Shafi'i rite; and the two main *tariiqas*, the Qaadiriya and Ahmadiya, are represented in both the north and south. Indeed, the Somali as a whole, and this should be emphasized, are highly orthodox and inclined to a fervent and deep attachment to their faith. The introduction of Islam can thus, I think, be assumed to be a fairly constant factor rather than a crucial variable in the present situation, and certainly there are no wide or systematic doctrinal differences between north and south.

In interpreting the different patterns of Islamic assimilation which have arisen in the two areas, therefore, we are forced to consider the effect of the differences in social structure and culture which distinguish these two segments of the Somali nation. In the following sections I outline briefly what seem the most significant variations in relation to the different patterns of Muslim assimilation which have resulted. I concentrate particularly on structural features, because they seem the most significant in the present context.

NORTHERN SOMALI SOCIAL STRUCTURE

While the entire Somali nation is embraced within a single national genealogy and Somali society as a whole is divided into groups on a basis of agnatic descent, there are important differences in lineage organization between the north and the south. In the north the basic political units are clans with varying populations perhaps of the order of 60,000 to 100,000 individuals. As befits a nomadic people, these units are not strictly localized; and without reference to locality clans are highly segmented internally into a wide array of subsidiary lineage groups. Of these segments within a clan, the most stable political unit is, as we have seen, the so-called '*dia*-paying group'.

Despite the extent to which the loyalties of the individual stockherder are bound tightly to his *dia*-paying group, the group has no formal organisation of authority. Generally, there is no single 'headman' with any authoritative functions, and all adult men have in principle an equal say in decision-making and policy-making. Indeed, the situation is such that lack of formally instituted political authority is a keynote of northern pastoral society. Moreover, with the premium which normally attaches to force as the ultimate sanction in group relations, strongly developed lineages are at a distinct advantage and enjoy a superior political status in relation to weaker collateral segments. Hence, the order of seniority by birth is not a factor of direct political significance in lineage relations, although first-born (*'urad*) lineage segments retain certain ceremonial duties in the veneration of common founding ancestors.

Although northern Somali political relations thus depend upon a combination of contractual with agnatic principles, and lineages provide the primary referents by which the individual identifies himself in relation to others, lineages are not normally corporate groups in a geographical sense. The pastures of northern Somaliland are regarded as a common gift to Somali nomads in general and are not conceived of as divided out among specific groups. Consequently, while lineages tend to exercise proprietorial rights to specific wells and trading centres, pastoral movement is wide-ranging and it is only extremely rarely that agnatic kinsmen live for any length of time together in a circumscribed territory. Generally in the pastures, camps of nomads and livestock belonging to different and often potentially hostile lineages intermingle, and prescriptive rights to territory are not asserted. At the same time, with the widespread use which is made of contractual alliance as a basis for political and legal collaboration at all levels of lineage structure, and not merely at the level of the most stable political aggregate which I have called '*dia*-paying group'[1], the combination of lineages by genealogical assimilation and manipulation which is so prominent a feature of other segmentary lineage societies is rare in northern Somaliland. The actual form of lineage pedigrees is thus apparently very largely a product of actual generation growth.[2] For the lineage identity which a person acquires at birth remains of vital significance throughout his life, and there is hardly any ambiguity about the genealogical (and hence social and political) placement of individuals or groups. And with the extreme emphasis which is thus given to agnatic descent as a basis for unfailing, though elastic and variable social bonds, marriage is viewed as a subsidiary source of social and quasi-political ties. Hence, ideally, one marries where one has already no strong agnatic ties, and marriage is preferentially directed outside the close circle of agnatic kin. Thus, marriage rarely takes place within the *dia*-paying groups; and the customarily preferential parallel-cousin marriage of Arab Muslims is not practised by most northern Somali nomads. In keeping with the social distance between affines, high bride-wealths and correspondingly high dowries are regularly exchanged. Nevertheless, marriage is unstable and divorce extremely frequent.[3]

The preceding is, necessarily, a very cursory summary of northern Somali social structure, but it will, I hope serve to bring out the points of difference which I wish to emphasize in relation to the southern Sab, to whom I now turn.

SOUTHERN SOMALI SOCIAL STRUCTURE

Southern Somali social structure exhibits a number of significant differences which can be summarized quickly, though inadequately, as follows. First, with their history of mixed origins, the southern Somali have a somewhat amorphous and certainly highly heterogeneous lineage structure. The maximum socio-political units here are essentially confederations of lineages – usually of disparate clan origins – united according to the stock explanation by a kind of act of union or 'promise' (balan) on the part of the original founding segments. These southern territorially based units, corresponding in size to the 'clans' of the north, differ again from the latter in also representing generally the standard locus of dia-paying solidarity in the south. They are not, as in the north, normally divided internally into a number of separate and autonomous dia-paying groups. These southern 'clans'[4] are, however, internally segmented on a putatively lineage pattern, and under the clan chief each internal section has a representative headman, the structure of authority paralleling that of internal subdivision. Externally, southern clans are loosely linked together, again on a putatively genealogical basis, in wider federations, but these larger associations do not act as corporate political groups.

This southern equivalent to the northern Somali clan is essentially a land-based unit, and frequently the names in its shallow quasi-genealogical framework refer directly to territorial sections rather than to genealogical segments in a true sense. The clan's arable resources are clearly demarcated from those of other similar units and distributed internally among its sections. Acquisitions of rights to arable land in the south thus requires, if a person is not already a member of a land-holding group, that he should seek admission as an adopted client in the clan of his choice. In return for receiving a grant of land for cultivation, the client has formally to undertake to accept joint responsibility with other members in the payment and receipt of all damages involving his clan of adoption. Normally clients are thus admitted after giving these undertakings and paying nominal gifts to the headman and clan chief.

Generally three classes of residents are distinguished: (a) descendants of the groups which were party to the original clan treaty; (b) long-standing accretions of diverse origin; and (c) recently adopted aliens. In addition, there were in the past often attached serfs of Oromo and Bantu origin, who performed much of the actual labour of cultivation. These last, however, have in the last few generations been progressively assimilated and appear today to enjoy rights to land similar to those held by other adopted clients, although a certain stigma still attaches to them. In practice, the present situation indeed is that although the dialect spoken by the southern Somali is that of the founding groups, it is extremely difficult to find any living Somali who can produce an authentic genealogy tracing descent from them. Thus, in reality, these cultivating clans seem to consist of layer upon layer of adopted clients in varying degrees of assimilation to an original founding core, which, over the generations has been swamped by subsequent accretions. So varied are these that there is no Somali clan or lineage of any size which is not represented among them. Some clans have something approaching what might be called a 'dominant lineage structure', but in general this is a very approximate and over-simplified way of characterizing the situation: and in keeping with this, genealogies are of very shallow depth compared with the north.

Yet in every one of these mixed units there is one section putatively associated with the original founders and referred to like the first-born segments of northern lineages as '*urad*. These segments play a special part in clan ritual, usually having the task of slaughtering animals in sacrifice, and seem to be those containing the most authentic descendants in each clan. They are not, however, 'first born' in a literal sense – as is generally recognized. Indeed, among the southern Somali in general the pattern of division of groups is not, as in the north, the outcome of uneven growth in a historical sense, but rather a reflection of the genealogical idiom in terms of which people and groups claim to be associated. And, apparently in keeping with this loose form of organization, with its lack of any firm fabric of agnatic kinship, marriage most frequently takes place within the bounds of *dia*-paying solidarity. Consistent with this, since marriage is here regarded as a means of strengthening weak existing ties, rather than as in the north of supplementing strong agnation, there is no objection to the characteristic pattern of Muslim patrilateral parallel-cousin marriage which, with matrilateral cross-cousin marriage, is practised preferentially (cf. Hellander, forthcoming). Bride-wealth and dowry, however, are small in comparison with the north, although there seems to be little difference in the high degree of marriage instability.

CULTIC VARIATIONS

A prominent aspect of Somali Islam generally is the power of intervention ascribed to Muslim saints as intermediaries between man and the Prophet and God. Here, as we have seen, three main categories of saints are recognized. There are first those great saints of Islam, particularly the founders of Qaadiriya and Ahmadiya *tariiqas*, who enjoy universal respect and veneration for the quality and strength of their *baraka* (mystical power) and *karamat* (miraculous works). Secondly, there are a large number of local Somali saints who are venerated for their own personal piety and works, and for the prominent part they have played in Somali Islam. The third and final group of saints consists of those Somalis who are venerated not, as in the previous category, for their known piety and blessing, but simply as the founders of lineage segments. These last are lineage ancestors who have in effect been canonized within Islam. Saints vary, of course, in the charismatic status accorded to them, and the most powerful, respected and best-known saints in the lineage ancestors class are the founders of large groups of clans. Typical of these are Sheikhs Daarood and Isaaq, founders of the Daarood and Isaaq families of clans in the north; and Sheikh Digil, putative founder of the southern Digil and Rahanwiin Somali. Here the degree of mystical power attributed to these saints corresponds directly to the numerical size of the groups which they represent, but varies inversely with the extent of social and political cohesion, which, at this high level of grouping, is minimal.

At a lower level of grouping, immediate differences are evident between the north and the south. In keeping with the strength of lineage ties among the northern nomads and the highly ramified character of their lineage system, every ancestor in the genealogies is in principle regarded as a saint and so venerated at periodical ceremonies in his honour. Among the southern Somali, however, where lineages have less vital functions, in place of the northern hierarchy of lineage saints one finds a proliferation of local saints honoured for their particular mystical powers. Typical of, and outstanding among these, is Sheikh Muumin, whom most of the Rahanwiin clans regard as the protector of their crops from attack by birds and other pests (see Ch. 6). Other similar saints, who also have no special lineage status, provide general security and blessing in all departments of life at the many shrines in the country occupied by the Sab.

Here then, clearly a degree of selection as between north and south occurs in the categories of saints who are most widely venerated, a selection which conforms to the differences in lineage organization already noted. But the effects of the differences in social structure between the northern nomads and their southern kinsmen extend beyond this. Among the northern pastoralists the characteristic religious expression of social identity at the level of the clan takes the form of an annual celebration (*siyaaro*) in praise of the clan ancestor. This is a typical memorial service performed regularly by other groups, larger and smaller, at other levels of lineage division.

In the south, however, the corresponding rite of clan identity is not a similar ceremony in honour of the putative group ancestors, but a collective rain-making ritual (*roobdoon*) held annually at a traditionally sacred centre. Here petitions are addressed directly to God, through the Prophet, without the intermediacy of ancestors, and in a definite order the several main subsections of the clan make animal offerings, praying for rain and prosperity in the coming year. Characteristically, the privilege of making the first offering belongs to the so-called '*urad* and genealogically most 'authentic' clan section. Rain-making in the north, by contrast, is not a collective clan rite in which the several divisions of a clan assert their corporate identity, but a generally ad hoc affair in which small groups of nomads encamped in the pastures pray to God to bring them rain as they see the clouds massing before the onset of the wet season.

These differences in corporate cult life clearly reflect the prevailing distinctions in lineage structure between north and south. But to avoid misunderstanding, it must again be emphasized that these distinctions in the characteristic forms of religious activity, associated with the contrast between northern and southern Somali social structure, are essentially variations within a common framework of orthodox Muslim assumptions, beliefs and practices. In the south, as in the north, the same or similar saints in other categories are venerated in the same fashion, and neither region asks more of its saints or imputes more power to them, thus leaving in both areas the unique position of God and his Prophet unchallenged. And this overall assimilation of Islam seems, as I have suggested above, to accord with the common Cushitic pre-Islamic substratum of beliefs, for the former existence of which there is evidence in both the north and the south.

But what is perhaps most striking, though less easy to characterize accurately, is a wider division of emphasis between the two groups of Somali which seems again to conform to the underlying differences of their socio-ecological circumstances. In the north especially, there is a very clear-cut ideal distinction between the spiritual and secular order which assumes concrete expression in the division which is made between 'men of God' (*wadaad*, the Somali equivalent of the Arabic Sheikh) and 'men of the spear' or 'warriors' (*waranleh*). In practice, as we have emphasised earlier, 'warriors' and priests rub shoulders together in the same lineages; and because of the exigencies of the nomadic life and social system, religious settlements of priests fully independent of the all-encompassing nomadic world have rarely been able to establish themselves. In reality, all men – men of God included, however reluctantly – remain finally subject to the bonds of common *dia*-paying group allegiance which afford the only sure source of security for person and property. In practice therefore, while the distinction between the two orders is theoretically maintained and is buttressed by the mystical power which is generally attributed to priests, the pastoral social system is in effect all-pervasive.

In the south the situation is rather different. Here separate and autonomous, and often powerful, religious communities of priests have been able to establish themselves in the arable regions and have played an important role in southern local politics. Here, moreover, even at an ideal level, the distinction between 'warriors' and priests is not so clearly defined, and priests are certainly allowed greater influence in clan politics than is the rule in the north. Indeed, some priestly sections have infiltrated into clan confederacies, where they have established themselves as priestly dynasties and the Arab title 'Sheikh' is in some cases applied in the south with a political as well as religious connotation. This has led to the involvement of the mystical powers of sheikhs in the political life of the southern Somali, especially in wars between clans, to an extent that is generally foreign to northern Somali.

Southern Somali society thus conveys the impression that in secular affairs, and inter-clan politics particularly, Muslim influence is more pervasive than it is in the north. Hence, the possibilities of wider agricultural settlement and the accompanying distinctive features of social organization appear to offer more receptive conditions for Islamic assimilation, such at least as to make the social conditions of the south conform in some respects more closely to those in other African Muslim societies than is the case among northern Somali. Here, surely, it is significant that in southern Somali society the favoured form of preferential parallel-cousin marriage is practised extensively in contrast to the position in the north. This tentative conclusion, however, is in no sense intended to suggest that the depth of Muslim piety is greater in the south than the north. This is something which is very hard to estimate objectively. My own impression, for what it is worth as the opinion of a non-Muslim observer, is that each in their own way are as devoted and fervent adherents of Islam.

Notes

1   For a fuller discussion of the role of *dia*-paying groups in northern Somali society and their highly relative and fluctuating character, see Lewis, 1961, pp. 161 ff.
2   This is discussed in detail in Lewis, 1961 and 1994.
3   For a more detailed discussion of Somali marriage and the factors affecting its stability, see Lewis, 1994.
4   For a number of reasons, particularly their territorial basis, it might be preferable to use the term 'tribe' here, but I have retained 'clan' to emphasise that the units under discussion represent the same level of grouping as northern Somali clans.

Chapter 6

KEEPING THE BIRDS AT BAY IN THE BAY AREA

RELIGIOUS SPECIALISATION AND AGRICULTURE

Although as we have just discussed, the southern agro-pastoral Somali apply the pervasive Somali distinction between men of God and 'warrior' laity (*wadaaddo iyo waranleh*) less rigorously than their northern pastoral countrymen, this nevertheless remains a fundamental principle of role attribution (usually rendered in the Bay region as *warshidde iyo waranshidde*).

Here, as elsewhere in Somalia, men of God are essentially viewed as mediators and intercessors in domestic, socio-political and religious contexts. Both among the pastoral nomads and the bay cultivators, their duties may include rain-making (*roob-doon*). But as explained in the previous chapter, throughout the southern Somali tribes with their heterogeneous clan composition, the most regular occasion for rain-making ritual is the annual clan (or tribal) collective solidarity ceremony, typically led by the 'first-born' segment (rather than by a man of God). This is the structural equivalent amongst the northern nomads of the annual commemorative ritual (*siyaaro*) in honour of an eponymous lineage ancestor. This is usually held at a traditional sacred centre, often the site at which the clan founders are said to have assembled to form the original alliance.

A more specialised local Bay region religious role, reflecting the predominantly agricultural economy, is that of demarcating and blessing plots of arable land by reciting chapters of the Koran – usually Suras 36 and 57 (the '*Yaasiin*' and '*Tabaarak*' – cf. Helander, 1986, 6).

A further specialisation, directly linked to cultivation, is that of protecting the crops from bird molestation by voracious clouds of tiny *quellos*. In the Bay region, this is actually a monopoly excercised by the Reer Sheikh Muumin, a lineage of saints based at Bur Hacaba.

SHEIKH MUUMIN'S ORIGINS

Sheikh Muumin's shrine lies a little to the south-east of Bur Hacaba, just off the old Bur Hacaba-Baidoa road near a large baobab tree. The shrine which has been reconstructed at various times consists (at least in 1962) of two buildings. One contains the tomb of sheikh Haran Madare; the other that of our eponymous saint, Sheikh Muumin and the grave of his son, Sheikh Nuur. This is a significant religious assemblage, since the Reer Sheikh Muumin seem to have supplanted the Haran Madare as pre-eminent religious figures in the Bay region about the time of the famous Ajuran Sultanate which dominated the lower Shebelle region in the sixteenth and seventeenth centuries. The Haran Madare are represented in old Somali oral traditions as a branch of the saintly Walamogge lineage descended, according to the same sources, from the famous Sheikh Husseen Baliale – the patron saint of the Islamic population of Ethiopia (Andrzejewski 1975; Braukamper 1977; Lewis 1980) (See also Ch. 8). Local tradition associates the expansion of the Elai clan confederacy with its three main divisions (the 'Three Stools') from Baidoa to Bur Hacaba with the active support of Sheikh Haran Madare and his sons, Sheikhs Nuuriye and Adan (both of whom are buried beside Haran Madare). The three are credited with having outwitted the tyrannical (Oromo) local ruler, 'Geedi Babo', whose infamous deeds and final overthrow figures so prominently in Bay oral tradition (cf. Bono, 1930; Cassanelli 1982, p.123). The latter appears in some traditional accounts as the local agent of the Ajuran sultan.

However this may be, the transfer from Haran Madare's religious hegemony to that of the Reer Sheikh Muumin would appear to coincide (perhaps fortuitously) with the collapse of the Ajuran sultanate. Whatever the actual historical circumstances (possibly involving religious rivalry), the transition between the two religious regimes is represented as a smooth, harmonious process. Haran Madare himself is said to have prophesied the coming of Sheikh Muumin, who, I was told, was in comparison to other saints 'as the moon is to the stars'. In common with many other saints, Sheikh Muumin had the capacity to fly. His origins, however, remain more obscure than those provided for Haran Madare. The most impressive account is that reported by Eugenio Bono (1930) who describes Sheikh Muumin as the '[patron] saint of the Elai'. According to this same account the saint's mother, Asha Osman of the Iska Shatto clan, was impregnated by a divine spirit and nine months later gave birth in Mogadishu to Sheikh Muumin 'Abdille ('God's slave'). After studying the Koran and completing his religious studies in Mogadishu, the saint was transformed into a bird and flew off to the land of the Rahanwiin. He flew first to Bur Heibe where he was chased away as a bird of ill-omen, and encountered the same hostile reception at his second port of call, Bur Jejis, among the Helleda. He then flew to Bur Hacaba where in contrast he was warmly received, as the saint whose coming had been foretold by Haran Madare. The saint then resumed his human form and received abundant gifts of livestock and cloth, promising in return to help the Elai with his divine grace. Three specific requests were made: to achieve victory over the Wardai (Oromo), to desalinize wells, and to drive away the birds which molested the ripening crops. All these he successfully accomplished. After other prodigious feats in Lugh and Mogadishu, Sheikh Muumin returned to Bur Hacaba where he died at the age of forty-seven years in 1773 according to Bono's informants. The same source gives the nineteenth day of Shaban as the annual commemoration festival (I was told the ritual was held on the eighteenth day of that month).

THE SAINT'S CONTEMPORARY ROLE

As far as I know, the earliest contemporary European reports on the Reer Sheikh Muumin are those of the Italian explorer Robecchi-Briccheti (1899) and his contemporary, the pioneer administrative officer-explorer Ugo Ferrandi (1903). The latter describes them as exerting powerful influence in the Bay area, extending to Lugh, based on their reputation for sorcery and the evil eye. By these means, according to Ferrandi, they exacted tribute, exploiting their ancestors' sanctity to impress ignorant people. In the same vein, Ferrandi also reports a derogatory myth of origin (frequently used by the Somali to discredit groups) according to which the Reer Sheikh Muumin descend from Hawiye holymen who disgraced themselves by eating fish[1] during a famine. Ferrandi's negative view is consistent with his attachment to the people of Lugh whose religious settlement at Bardera had been under attack (unsuccessful it seems) by Reer Sheikh Muumin.

In any event, Bono's more favourable account (1930) tallies with what I found at Bur Hacaba some thirty years later. The Reer Sheikh Muumin, marrying endogamously and split into three sections were dispersed into three settlements at Mogadishu, Lugh and Bur Hacaba with a total population of about a thousand souls. According to Sheikh Muhammad Amin, the lineage's 'Capo-Qabiila' [from It. *clan chief*], the Reer Sheikh Muumin as a whole were the adherents of the Qaadiriya *tariiqa* and the eponymous saint had lived twelve generations previously (this is consistent with Bono's 1930 report of eleven generations).

The specialised crop protection rituals are conducted as follows. Each year, the head of the lineage posts an individual member of the group to sit in a small house (*aqal*) beside the baobab tree, close to Sheikh Muumin's tomb, to read the Koran from beginning to end to prevent birds attacking the crops. When the new Spring growth is a few inches high, the *Capo-Qabiila* visits the Elai chiefs and tells them whom he has designated to read the Koran in that season. The nomadic tent (*aqal*) is built by the Elai, each of the three Elai sections (or 'stools') taking it in turn to provide this facility (in 1962 when I was there it was the turn of the Geedafadde). The duty Sheikh stays for three months in the hut reading the Koran, and Elai farmers bring him supplies as *siyaaro*.

On the day that construction of the reading house begins, an ox and a sheep are sacrificed. When the building is complete but before the saintly reader takes up his position, each of the seven Elai chiefs, I was told, produces an ox for slaughtering. When the Sheikh enters his house to commence his work he is given three cows as a personal reward – one from each of the three Elai 'seats' (i.e. clan sections) as well as being supplied on a daily basis with milk and ghee. The Koran is then read, according to my informant, twice for each of the three Elai 'seats' and once more (a seventh time) for the clan section responsible for building the house in a particular year. In keeping with the myth of the saint's initially hostile reception by the neighbouring Helleda and Eyle, although these clans come 'for blessing' the Koran is not read for their fields: this is a privilege accorded only to the three Elai seats. The seven readings correspond neatly with the general value of the figure seven in Islamic cultures (as for example in the duration of the marital 'honey-week' – cf. honeymoon) and more specifically to seven-day rain-making ceremonies conducted by Sheikh Muumin (cf. Helander, 1984).[2]

NATURAL AND SACRED FERTILITY

Thus, in this southern cultivating region in addition to the routine intercessory and mystically productive roles of saints (including rain-making) elsewhere in Somalia, we find a regional specialisation – crop-protection – reflecting the requirements of the local economy. Although they appear to remain unreported in the literature, it would seem likely that other saintly families must be expected to provide similar protective services in other cultivating districts and I have heard of at least one instance of this in the north-west (Borama

District) where cultivation is, of course, much more recent (Ahmad Farrah, personal communication). It seems logically consistent with their reputation as mystical 'scarecrows', that the farmers of the Bay area should also look to the Reer Sheikh Muumin to control the time of harvest. According to my informants, the crops should not be cut until farmers have reported to the incumbent Sheikh that the grain is ripe, and he has authorized that the harvest should proceed. Thus, through blessing the earth and those who labour on it, facilitating the rains, protecting the growing crop, and regulating the time of harvesting, in mystical terms the Reer Sheikh Muumin certainly seem to control production and reproduction in the Bay region.

According to the local ideology, the mystical efficacy of the Reer Sheikh Muumin depends directly on the *baraka* of the saintly eponym (virgin-born according to the myth recorded by Bono). This is tangibly displayed in the votive offering-strewn shrine and tomb itself juxtaposed with that of the earlier mystically charged Haran Madare. Since celibacy is not a pre-condition for fecund mystical power in this context, and indeed the sexuality of saints is extremely highly charged, I am not convinced by Bernhard Helander's (1984) ingenious structuralist argument that sexual abstinence releases mystically charged energy to fructify the crops whereas human growth is promoted by sexual activity in the absence of religion. In the local view again, whether through the grace of Sheikh Muumin or other mediators, religious blessing is ultimately a precondition for successful human reproduction. Infertility and other reproductive disorders are amongst the commonest motives which bring people to Sheikh Muumin's shrine in search of blessing. No wonder the tomb is so festooned with votive offerings – promissory strings, threads, pieces of cloth and even, when I visited it, two razor blades symbolizing the supplicant's intention to kill an ox for the saints once his petition for fertility had been granted. Of course, at a more abstract level, I would argue that, universally, human sexuality provides a powerful prototype for the release of transcendent mystical energy (cf. Lewis 1971, 1977).

Notes

1 The eating of fish has negative connotations for some Somali, particularly nomads.

2 Helander's discussion centres on the legendary rain-making expertise of Sheikh Muumin whom he describes as a Sufi saint of the 'Saalihiya Order' who died some twenty years ago. Muumin is locally an understandably popular name, and it may thus be that Helander is referring to some other personage

Chapter 7

THE 'BLESSED SAINT', SHARIF YUUSUF BARKHADLE OF THE WORLDS

SHARIF YUUSUF'S MISSIONARY ROLE

The most powerful and widely celebrated local saint in the centre of northern Somaliland is Sharif Yuusuf Barkhadle, whose shrine lies near the dry river bed of Dogor, some twenty miles to the north-east of the provincial capital of Hargeisa. Sharif Yuusuf, also known as Yuusuf al-Ikwaan ('Yuusuf of the Brethren') and as Yuusuf al-Kawnayn ('Yuusuf of the Worlds'), is popularly credited with the introduction of the Arabian type black-headed, fat-tailed sheep which is the main variety bred today in the area. But he is most widely remembered amongst the Somali as one of the principal early teachers of Islam and as the inventor of a Somali notation for the Arabic short vowels which helped to facilitate the teaching of Arabic[1]. Today, his shrine near Dogor is regularly visited by pilgrims in search of blessing and fertility and is the scene of an annual memorial feast held on the first Friday (known as *jima'a Barkhadle*) of the dark phase of the moon in the Muslim month of *jumada al-awwal*. To the majority of Somali it is as 'Barkhadle' , the Blessed One, that he is best known, and his mystical prominence is indicated by the popular belief that to visit his tomb three times has the same religious value as going once on pilgrimage to Mecca. The celebration of his birthday service is one of the main events in the religious calendar in northern Somaliland, and with 'Abdul Qaadir Jiilani he is the only saint so regularly honoured in this part of Somaliland.

Sharif Yuusuf is also associated in the local oral tradition with the rulers of the Muslim state of Adal, and with the jihads of that period against the Christian Abyssinian kingdom: indeed some Somalis appear to believe that the 'hidden *Imam*' will one day appear from the saint's tomb and lead them to victory. This traditional connection with the Muslim dynasties of Ifat and Adal is also suggested by the site of the shrine, for it is surrounded by walled mounds and other remains of what seems once to have been a walled town. This site has not yet been the subject of archaeological excavation, but it appears likely that it should be grouped with the series of mediaeval ruined cities surveyed by Curle in 1934[2]. Like Aw Barkhadle[3], two other ruined towns in this group – Aw Barre and Aw Bube – are similarly named after local saints. The earliest dates at which these often considerable settlements were founded has still to be determined, for, in fact, not a single one of these important sites has yet been systematically excavated. Pottery and coin finds, obtained by Curle during his surveys, indicate, however, that the majority of these centres flourished in the fifteenth and sixteenth centuries, which takes us up to the time of Ahmad Granhe's death in 1542 and the collapse of the Muslim conquests.

Quite independently, on the basis of an apparent reference to Sharif Yuusuf in the Harar chronicles, Dr. E. Cerulli has suggested that Yuusuf Barkhadle may be identified with one of the ancestors of the Walashma dynasty of Ifat,[4] and additional evidence to this effect is furnished by a further version of this Harar king-list of the rulers of Adal which I collected in 1956 and discuss below. Finally, northern Somali oral tradition also claims that in the course of his missionary wars Yuusuf Barkhadle visited the southern Somali area with a party of his disciples. In the course of my research in the south of the Somali Republic in 1962, I discovered local traditions corroborating these northern claims and repeating in slightly different versions one of the most notable of his miracles to which reference is made below.

THE SHARIF'S EXALTED ORIGINS

It will be as well to begin this account of Sharif Yuusuf with the record[5] conserved by the custodians of his shrine concerning his divinely inspired mission to spread the light of Islam in Somaliland. As the Prophet was dying, it is related, he spoke with 'Ammar B. Yasir[6], foretelling the life of Sharif Yuusuf and his miraculous works. The Prophet told 'Ammar that there would come one created by God and with the Prophet's own light, whom God would exalt and who would be called Kawnayn. He would inherit the Prophet's own long robe, Solomon's ring, Moses' stick, and a blessed stone. He would be born in 666 AH. (1266/7 AD)[7] and would meet 'Ammar in Baghdad on a Friday between noon and evening. He would come to

'Ammar's house riding a she-camel and carrying a milking vessel. When the Sheikh came, the Prophet told 'Ammar he was to return his greeting and give him the relics entrusted to his keeping. Then 'Ammar would die. Sheikh Yuusuf himself would be buried in the land of the *barbari*, having been sent there to guide those people in the right path and to rectify their sins. His blessing would be such that to see him once would be worth 660 years of prayer. At first in his missionary endeavour, however, Sharif Yuusuf would meet with hostility; but once it was seen how wondrous were his works he would be respected and those who honoured him would prosper in both worlds. He who respected the Sheikh, God would also honour; and those who despised him God would reject. His prayers would be answered and his blessings would enrich the land and its people until they forgot his words and fell into evil ways, fighting and bloodshed.

Such were the miraculous gifts given to this man of God that he would be learned without learning; all mankind and jinns in such number as to fill the space between the earth and sky, would be placed at his disposal. Those who visited Sharif Yuusuf would visit God. Hence the final advice: 'Behold and always guard his image in your heart. He who denies Sharif Yuusuf's blessing denies the mighty works of God. We place our trust in God's protection and hope that we may not deny his blessing. There are some men who love each other for God's sake, and not on account of considerations of wealth and tribal connection. Their faces are full of light and they do not know fear. God directs to the right path those who please Him.'

SHARIF YUUSUF AND THE HISTORY OF ADAL

With such powerful reference to this apocryphal tradition ascribed to the Prophet, the blessings and efficiency of Sharif Yuusuf are validated for the custodians of his shrine and for those who make pilgrimage there. The attendants at the tomb, however, know little beyond this of his history. They give his genealogy as: Sharif Yuusuf Barkhadle b. Ahmad b. Mahammad b. 'Abdillahi b. Isma'il b. Musa b. Huseyn b. 'Ali b. Hamza b. Qasim b. Yahya b. Huseyn b. Ahmad b. Quwayi b. Yahya b. 'Ise b. Mahammad b. Taqi al-Hadrama b. 'Abdul b. Hadi b. Mahammad b. 'Ali b. Musa b. Ja'far b. Mahammad b. 'Ali b. Hasan 'Ali Talib. Like many other *Ashraf* immigrants in Somaliland he is thus regarded as of Quraysh origin.

In this genealogy the saint's descendants are not given and no precise connection with the rulers of Ifat is shown. However, in the following short king-list of the 'Rulers of the land of Sa'd ad-Din' which I collected in 1956 at Borama and which was said to have been copied from an old work by Sharif Ibraahim, Yuusuf is identified as one of the ancestors of this line of Muslim kings. The text translates as follows:

'Then came into office 'Umar b. Dunyahur b. Ahmad b. Maham-mad b. Hamid b. Sheikh Yuusuf al-Ikhwaan, nicknamed 'Bark-hadle', b. Mahammad b. 'Abdillahi b. Sa'id b. 'Ali b. Mahammad b. Isma'il b. Yahya al-Qurayshi, al Hashimi, a descendant of Hasan b. 'Ali b. Abi Talib, *May God bless his countenance!* He was followed by his son Burfawe (for ten years), then by his brother Haqq ad-Din Nas-rawi (for seven years). These chosen four are his sons. Then came into office Mansur b. Burnawe (for five years), then Jamal ad-Din b. Burnawe (for seven years). He was learned and concerned for the well-being of his people: he had jinn servants. For each day there was a jinn who used to bring him a letter from Abawein in one hour. The water used to come to him from a river called the Awash.

'He was succeeded by Abuta (for two years), then Zubayr (for two years). After her came Sabr ad-Din (for five years). Then Qat 'Ali (for forty years), then his son 'Ar'ad (for two years). At this time the *hijera* was 787. Then came his son Haqq ad-Din b. Harb 'Ar'ad (for ten years). He died a martyr. He was the man who organized the means of waging the holy war. Then followed him Sultan Sa'd ad-Din b. Ahmad in the month of *safar* in the year 788 and he died a martyr in *dhul-hijera* of the year 817. He ruled for twenty-seven years (*sic.*), ten months and five days. After him came Sabr ad-Din b. Sa'd (for eight-een years). And then there was an interval of over one year because they were in Arabia for about two years and several months. They stayed in the country they visited for two years and then the date was 825 AH. Then came his brother Mansur b. Sa'd ad-Din (for ten years and seven months; some people say it was for seven years, but God knows best!) Then came Sultan Jamal ad-Din b. Sa'd ad-Din in 835 AH. (for seven years) and he was killed as a martyr on the 24th day of the month of *jumada al-awwal*, 836. Next succeeded Sultan Badlay b. Sa'd ad-Din (for thirteen years and twenty-four days), and he was killed on the late afternoon of 26th Ramadan in the year 849 and he ruled for twenty-six years. Afterwards his son 'Umar suc-ceeded him: but God knows best and this copy has been extracted from an old book by Sharif Ibrahim'.

In this chronicle, Sharif Yuusuf, identified as the saint most gener-ally known to Somali as Yuusuf al-Ikhwaan, or Barkhadle, appears as the fifth ascending ancestor of 'Umar b. Dunyahur, the founder of the Walashma dynasty. From the dates given it appears that 'Umar

b. Dunyahur's reign ended in 698 AH. Hence if we allow a period of twenty-five years for each generation, Sharif Yuusuf himself presumably died about 1190 AD In the much fuller history of the Walashma dynasty published by Cerulli[8], of which the foregoing seems to be but a copied fragment, the saint is simply styled Yusuf Barkhadle and figures as the fifth ascending ancestor of 'Umar b. Dunyahuz (Dunyahur, in my version). In this version of the chronicle the latter's reign is given as terminating in 687 AH. It is not unlikely that this and other discrepancies between the two texts are due to errors by the copyist and it is therefore reassuring to find some independent indication of the period of 'Umar Dunyahuz's reign in the Shoan history chronicle discovered by Cerulli in Harar in 1936[9]. In this text, reference is made to 'Ali b. Wali Asma as having fired Walalah, capital of the Muslim state of Shoa in the year 676 AH. and the successful incorporation of the state under the rule of the Walashma dynasts of Adal by 688 AH. (1289 AD)[10].

It thus seems possible to locate Sharif Yuusuf as the fifth or sixth ascending ancestor of 'Umar b. Dunyahuz (Walashma) in the twelfth century. In the absence of archaeological excavations it is, of course, not yet possible to know whether the ruined town associated with the saint's tomb at Dogor also belongs to this period. However, as we have seen, remains from the other similar ruined cities of the area indicate that they flourished up to the fifteenth and sixteenth centuries. And already in the sixteenth century Sharif Yuusuf's shrine was apparently an important holy place since, in another Harar chronicle, the tarikh al-mujahidin, first published by Paulitschke[11] and also discussed by Cerulli, reference is made to the death of the Garaad Jibril (who led a revolt against the reigning Emir of Harar, 'Uthman) in 1569, and to his burial in 'the place of the great saint known as Aw Barkhadle'[12].

SHARIF YUUSUF'S BLESSINGS

There thus seems every reason to regard Sharif Yuusuf as one of the ancestors of the Walshma dynasty of Ifat. For the majority of those who now live in Northern Somaliland and come on pilgrimage to his tomb, however, this is not the connection which excites most interest. Rather, in this region dominated by the powerful Isaaq group of clans, interest centres on the assumed connection between the saint and their own clan eponym, Sheikh Isaaq, whose grave lies several hundred miles further to the east at Mait on the Erigavo coast. Often the two saints are regarded popularly as having lived about the same time, an equation which, while mirroring their contemporary ritual significance today, may also have some historical validity; this view is at least in broad agreement with the picture which can be pieced together from traditional accounts of the expansion and migration of the Isaaq clans from Mait about the twelfth century[13]. Since, however, Aw Barkhadle's precise connection with the rulers of Ifat is not widely known, he appears as an isolated figure, and in comparison with the million or so spears of the Isaaq lineage, a saint deprived of known issue. This striking difference between these two saints is explained in a popular legend, according to which, when Sheikh Isaaq and Aw Barkhadle met, the latter prophesied that Isaaq would be blessed by God with many children. He, however, would not have descendants, but Isaaq's issue would pay him respect and *siyaaro* (voluntary offerings). So it is, one is told, that every year the Isaaq clansmen gather at Aw Barkhadle's shrine to make offerings in his name.

Sharif Yuusuf also figures prominently in a widely known legend which validates the current Somali practice of giving small gifts to the Yibir itinerant soothsayers who come to bless newly-married couples and newly-born children. These dispersed Yibir, who cannot today number more than perhaps a few thousand persons, are the numerically smallest group of those traditionally despised artisan specialists who are attached to mainstream Somali groups as bondsmen, and known collectively as *sab*.[14] In conformity with their numerical and political insignificance as a group, as I have argued elsewhere[15], these Yibir bondsmen enjoy a formidable reputation for sorcery, cursing, and other malevolent acts. Despite their traditional attachment to particular Somali clans and lineages, they conserve their own pedigrees, tracing descent ultimately from a founding ancestor known pejoratively as Bu'ur Ba'ayer, or Mahammad Hanif. The story goes that when Sharif Yusuf came to Somaliland and settled near the site of his eventual burial place, he was met by the Yibir leader and ancestor who then ruled the country, in many respects contrary to the law of Islam. The two leaders then decided that the struggle for legitimacy between them should be by a trial of mystical strength. Sharif Yuusuf accordingly challenged Mahammad Hanif to pass through a small hill which rises beside Dogor. This miracle the Yibir ancestor twice accomplished successfully, but in the middle of his third demonstration of his powers, Sharif Yuusuf invoked the superior might of God and imprisoned his rival for ever within the mountain. Thus orthodox Islam prevailed, and the Yibirs were defeated. Mahammad Hanif's descendants, however, so the story goes, claimed blood compensation from Sharif Yuusuf's followers for all time to come, and this is the origin and practice of the gifts regularly made to Yibirs.

The extent of the Sheikh's reputation for mystical power is

indicated by the fact that a similar tale is told in southern Somalia. Thus, in the Baidoa area I found in 1962 that Sharif Yuusuf – known here as Konton Barkhadle ('the fifty times blessed') – was said to have resolved a similar confrontation with non-Muslim Oromo in the same fashion. Sharif Yuusuf, tradition holds, entered the region with a large party of students only to meet the Oromo leader called Qanana and his followers. Sharif Yuusuf was asked what he had come for; and when he answered that he had come to teach Islam and bring blessings, he was asked to give proof of his powers. Sharif Yuusuf responded, it is said, by pointing out that his adversaries were better equipped in men and in arms and should therefore prove their powers first. Qanana, on this challenge, passed twice through a mountain. On his third attempt, however, Sharif Yusuf imprisoned him for ever by reciting the *sura al-Yasin*.

In another tradition still current today in the Baidoa area, Sharif Yuusuf is also connected with a sharif called Mahammad Qiyas-je'el, belonging to the Gardere Somali clan, who with three others is reputed to have provided the original nucleus of the Wanjil clan.[16] The story goes that Sharif Mahammad was one of those students who sat at the feet of Sharif Yuusuf as he, each day, distributed food amongst his followers. All the students took their share of the roasted coffee beans (*bun*) provided by the Sharif, but each day one of the itinerant school died. Sharif Muhammad, noticing this persuaded his colleagues always to leave a little food aside for Sharif Yusuf. Then the deaths stopped, and Sharif Yuusuf gave the name 'Qiyas je-el' (lit. 'a good sharing') to Sheikh Mahammad. Today, in memory of this example, when people eat roasted coffee beans, or other food, it is common to leave a little over. And that is the origin of this table etiquette.

In contrast to the story of Mahammad Hanif and his Yibir descendants, as far as I know, no contemporary groups of the region claim descent from Qanana, and the tale of Qanana's being locked in the mountain is not linked to any practice of gift-giving by anyone. But it is interesting that the stories of Sharif Yuusuf should exist in an area almost five hundred miles from his shrine and amongst people who have scarcely any contact with northern Somaliland, and who speak a different and not fully mutually intelligible dialect of Somali. The occurrence of the miracle legends here, I believe, suggests that Sharif Yuusuf did in fact visit this part of Somaliland in the course of his missionary work, thus corroborating the oral tradition current in northern Somaliland of the Sharif's travels in the south. His contact with Oromo in this area in the twelfth century adds further support to Cerulli's conclusions drawn from other traditional sources as to the presence of Oromo groups in this area prior to the Somali.[17]

PILGRIMAGE AT THE SHARIF'S SHRINE

The shrine of Aw Barkhadle is at Dogor some twenty miles to the
north-east of Hargeisa[18]. The present white-washed domed tomb
was built in the 1920s by an Indian contractor, at the instigation of
Sheikhs Mahammad and Said 'Abdulla Isaaq (of the Habar Yunis
clan) the then heads of the family who are the traditional custodians
of the shrine. Beside the shrine a *hanun* bush (*Suaedia fruticosa*) is covered with small strips of cloth and pieces of string, hung there as
votive offerings. Not far from the tomb lie the ruins of a large Friday
mosque which is said to have been used in the life-time of the Sharif.
The tomb itself occupies much of the shrine and is covered with an
embroidered red and green cloth which visitors touch reverently
with the palms of their hand – which they then kiss – for it is
believed to be strongly permeated with *baraka*. A number of relics are
also conserved. One of these is an old Koran, said to have been written by Sharif Yuusuf himself, and bound in gold-tooled leather.
Another relic is a piece of wood, said to be a leg of the saint's own
bed. It is believed that if this is touched by a barren woman it will
enable her to bear children, and by touching it a pregnant woman
may avoid a miscarriage. There was also, I was told, another relic in
the form of four stones bound together in the shape of a cross. This
was said to have been stolen by some visiting pilgrims a generation
ago. It was used to treat impotence, apparently being placed on the
penis of those so afflicted.

The annual visitation (*siyaaro*) ceremony is held on the first Friday
of the dark period of the month of *jumada al-awwal*. Pilgrims from all
over the northern regions of the country assemble on the preceding
days, many arriving by lorry. Several thousand normally gather
together and large numbers of livestock are killed for feasting on the
Thursday night (the start of the Muslim Friday). The rejoicing continues late into the night and is accompanied by the singing of *qasidas* in praise of the saint, and much drumming. On the following
morning the pilgrims walk up the hill in which the Yibir ancestor is
supposed to be buried, some praying, and others daubing their fore-
heads with clay. Women, especially, pick up lumps of clay to take to
their homes. At the same time a regular stream of people files
through the shrine, round his tomb, touching it reverently in the
hope of gaining blessing. Shortly after mid-day all the pilgrims
assemble in a clearing which is bedecked with flags and banners,
and the Friday prayer is held, usually directed by the chief Kadi. This
is the end of the ceremony, which, ideally, should be blessed with

rain, and the pilgrims, tired after their long vigil but in a state of spiritual exhaltation, disperse.[19]

Notes

1 Thus, *alif* with *fatha* is known as *alif la kordabay* (lit. *alif* which is surmounted); *alif* with *kasra* is represented in Somali as *alif la hoosdabay* (lit. *alif* which is undercut); *alif* with *damma*, as *alif la goday* (lit. *alif* which is hollowed out); and *alif* with *sukun*, as *alif la rabbay* (lit. *alif* shortened). Cf. I.M. Lewis, 'The Gadabuursi Somali script', *BSOAS*, 1958, XXI, p.135.

2 A.T. Curle, 'The Ruined Towns of Somaliland', *Antiquity*, 1937, pp. 315-3327.

3 The title *Aw* is that customarily applied by Somali to a holy man.

4 *Documenti Arabi per la Storia dell'Etiopia*, 1931, p. 31.

5 This is written in a manuscript hagiology which does not seem to be of great antiquity.

6 This is one of the companions of the Prophet who died in 657 AD.

7 But see below, p. 89. This date is the same told to Burton in 1854 as that when Sayyid Yusuf ('al-Baghdadi') came to a place called Siyaro, near Berbera. See R.F. Burton, First Footsteps in Eastern Africa, Everyman edition, 1943, p. 82.

8 Cerulli, cit., 1931, pp. 4-15.

9 'Il Sultanato dello Scioa nel secolo XIII secondo un nuovo documento storico', RSE, 1941.

10 *Ibid.*, pp. 10, 12. Trimingham, *Islam in Ethiopia, 1952, p. 59 gives the date of 'Umar b. Dunyahuz's death at 1275/6.*

11 *Harar, Frschungreise nach den Somal-und Galla-Landern Ost-Afrikas*, Leipzig, 1888.

12 Cerulli, cit., 1931, p.67.

13 Cf. Lewis, 'The Galla (Oromo) in Northern Somaliland', RSE, 1959, pp. 21-38; 'Historical Aspects of Genealogies in Northern Somaliland', *JAH*, 1962, pp. 35-48.

14 Cf. Lewis, *A Pastoral Democracy*, 1961, p.14.

15 Lewis, 'Dualism in Somali Notions of Power', *JRAI*, 1963, pp. 109-116.

16 The Wanjil are a small mixed clan, partly of 'pre-Hawiye' origin (cf. M. Colucci, *Principi di diritto consuetudinariodella Somalia meridionale*, 1924, p. 139) situated near Baidoa and today attached to the Rahanwiin of the region.

17 E. Cerulli, 'Le popolazioni della Somalia nella tradizione storica locale', RRAL, 1926, pp. 150-172: cf. Lewis, *The Modern History of Somaliland*, 1965, pp. 22-28.

18 Another shrine for the saint, a *maqam*, to which similar pilgrimages are made in the west of the country is a large black stone at Qoranyale, near Borama. Here Sharif Yuusuf is said to have stopped for a time in the course of his missionary work in the west.

19 On one of the three occasions on which I participated, I suddenly found myself confronted by a swirling figure wielding an impressive sword.

Luckily for me, this man who appeared to be in a high state of religious excitement and was dountless affronted by the presence in this context of a pagan (*gaal*), was promtly seized by a well-known local elder who calmed my would-be assailant, enabling me to retreat safely.

Chapter 8

NATIONALISM AND THE MULTI-ETHIC LEGACY OF SHEIKH HUSSEEN OF BALE

The present, according to Collingwood's famous phrase, encapsulates the past. Although its history has still to be written, from what information is available it is becoming increasingly clear that this relationship between past and present is demonstrated with remarkable clarity in the case of the Western Somali Liberation Front (WSLF). Despite its title, this organization enjoyed in the 1970s a significant and probably strategically crucial following amongst the Muslim Oromo in Bale. Oromo support was by no means limited to Bale, but extended within the command structure of the movement in the Somali Ogaden, where the second-in-command was an Oromo. The WSLF was thus an alliance of Somali and Oromo Muslims, based on their close ethnic associations as Cushitic-speakers, common Islamic allegiance and mutual opposition to Amhara domination. This contemporary activation of old ethnic ties against the Christian and Semitic-speaking Amhara, gave rise to the expressions 'Abo-Somali' (Oromo) and 'Wariiya Somali' (Somali). These designations, based on the standard cries for attention in the two languages (equivalent to the shout 'Hey, you!') were employed to emphasise the common ethnic identity of the two groups.[1] This was also achieved genealogically by assimilating the Oromo in the Somali national genealogy as descendants of Irir, ancestor of the Hawiye and Dir Somali clan-families (cf. Colucci, 1924; Lewis, 1955, 1957, 1961).

In this chapter I shall argue that behind these dramatic contemporary developments loomed the powerful figure of the famous Sheikh Husseen of Bale, a multifaceted symbol of local Islamic (and anti-Christian Amhara) identity, bringing together Oromo, Somali and Arab elements. With this nationalist potential resonating down the centuries, Sheikh Husseen appears in retrospect as a Cushitic

time-bomb in the Ethiopian powder-keg. Sheikh Husseen has deep
roots in Somalia as well as Ethiopia. This Somali connection, despite
local transformations of Sheikh Husseen's cult, provided the most
pervasive historical context for the recent Oromo-Somali alliance in
(and also outside) the WSLF. So far as I am aware, however, this web
of historical connections which could, potentially, be invoked as a
charter for contemporary action, was ignored by the WSLF whose
leadership particularly stressed the secular origins and aims of their
movement.

THE ORIGINS OF THE WESTERN SOMALI LIBERATION FRONT

Two major strands can be traced in the brief history of the WSLF, a
movement organized under this name in 1975, with the objective of
recovering Somali sovereignty in the Ethiopian-occupied Somali
territories. The area involved extends northwards through the
Ogaden to the Awash river, including the land round Harar and
Dire Dawa inhabited by Somalis of the 'Iise and Gadabuursi clans.
Its southwards limits in Bale province of Ethiopia are less clearly
defined. This partly reflects the fluid character of Somali-Muslim
Oromo (especially Arusi) ethnicity – a matter which may well turn
out to be of crucial significance.

Following the Front's name (in some ways reminiscent of Djibou-
ti's old title 'French Somali Coast'), I shall first trace the Somali
strand in the events which led to the formation of the movement.
Modern organised Somali resistance to Ethiopian rule in the
Ogaden dates back to the 19th century, when Amhara expansion
into the region helped to precipitate the anti-Christian (and anti-
colonial) jihad waged from 1900 to 1920 by the fiery Ogaadeen
Sheikh, Mahammad 'Abdille Hassan. This began and ended in the
Ogaden. The next phase of Somali resistance to the Ethiopian pres-
ence in the Ogaden was in the1940s, immediately following the lib-
eration of Ethiopia from the Italians by the Allied Forces during the
Second World War and the ensuing British Military Administration.
In 1942 there were disturbances in the Harar-Jigjiga region con-
nected with Ethiopian attempts to impose taxation on the local
Somali population. In 1944, Ogaadeen clan leaders petitioned the
British Military Administration requesting Britain not to abandon
them to Ethiopian rule. In 1947 Britain was formally requested by
representatives of the clans involved to convey their views to the
United Nations.

With the failure of the Bevin Plan for Somali re-unification, the

Ogaden was formally transferred to Ethiopian rule in September 1947, and the same fate overtook the remaining northern Haud region (the so-called 'Reserved-Areas') in 1954 (see Lewis 1965, pp. 129 ff.; pp. 150 ff.). The latter action led to the formation in the British Somaliland Protectorate of the National United Front which, with representatives of the Ogaadeen clan, sought, unsuccessfully to take the Somali case to the International Court. Thus, when the independent state of Somalia was formed in 1960 by the union of the former British and Italian territories, the issue still rankled, and successive Somali governments were pledged to continue the campaign for re-unification. In 1960 a series of violent incidents occurred in the Danot area of the Haud, and a Somali guerrilla movement (known originally as *Nasrullahi* – God's Grace), led by Makhtar Dahir soon developed. These bitter clashes between Ethiopian troops and Somali clansmen quickly escalated, leading in March 1964 to a brief outburst of fighting between the armed forces of Ethiopia and the Somali Republic. Following the restoration of peace between the two neighbouring states, the Ogaadeen insurgent movement lost momentum and went underground. The Ethiopian Third Division was stationed in the Ogaden to hold the region. After a period of imprisonment, Makhtar left Ethiopia in 1962. The Somali campaign was diverted to another front, that in northern Kenya where the Somali nationalist guerrillas, known to the Kenyans disparagingly as *shifta* (bandits), took to arms to pursue their claims for self-determination.

Meanwhile, to the south in Bale province, a parallel Oromo insurgence quickly developed. This was again directed at the Amhara administration in the area and was led by an Oromo war-lord called Wako Guto (whom I met in Mogadishu in the 1970s). Fighting started in 1963 and continued until 1970 when massive Ethiopian military action re-established Ethiopian government authority, and Wako Guto made peace with Emperor Haile Selassie, even receiving the title of *Dejazmatch* (see Aberra Ketsela, 1971).

In the course of this protracted struggle, many Arusi, Borana and other Oromo guerrillas and civilians sought refuge from the attacking Ethiopian forces by crossing into Somalia. Although many received charitable treatment from the civilian Somali population, their presence was embarrassing to the Somali government which, from 1967, under the premiership of Mahammad Haji Ibrahim Egal, was seeking to establish cordial relations with Ethiopia and Kenya. General Siyad Barre's military regime, which seized power in October 1969, continued this policy and found it prudent to imprison some of the Oromo nationalist leaders, including Sheikh Jarra, a leader of the Oromo Liberation Front in Harar and Bale.

The new military regime which ousted Haile Selassie's government in Ethiopia in September 1974 soon attempted to impose its rule throughout the state. The effect of this brutal intervention of centralist autocracy was to encourage the growth of regional autonomist movements in Ethiopia, and to rekindle the fires of established nationalist movements, especially in Eritrea, the Ogaden and Bale. This new experience of direct rule promoted the merger of previously separate guerrilla organizations. Thus Wako Guto who had moved from Bale to Somalia in 1975, returned in 1976 to organize the WSLF movement there. And Sheikh Jarra, who had spent five years in prison in Somalia, was released to organise the allied Oromo Liberation Front operating round Harar. The official WSLF, with its fifteen man committee, operated in the Ogaden under joint Somali-Oromo leadership. The two strands of eastern-Ethiopian dissent were tightly interwoven, with Islam cementing ethnic affinity. Retrospectively, it can now be seen how these contemporary developments derive naturally from the cult of Sheikh Husseen of Bale which, over the centuries, has served both to promote the expansion of Islam and the fusion of Somali and Oromo ethnicity in this region.

THE CULT OF SHEIKH HUSSEEN OF BALE IN ETHIOPIA

As is well-known, the shrine of Sheikh Husseen in the Goba plain in Bale is the most important Muslim centre of pilgrimage in southern Ethiopia (cf. Cerulli, 1931, 1933, 1938, etc.; Trimingham, 1952; Andrzejewski, 1972, 1974a, 1974b, 1975). The Sheikh's annual festival held on February 7th attracts huge crowds of pilgrims from regions as distant as Wollega, northern Kenya and southern Somalia. It is probably not an exaggeration to say that in the 1970s particularly, Sheikh Husseen had become the patron saint for all Muslims in this region. As the spiritual residue, so to speak, of the ancient Muslim state of Bale (for a valuable discussion of this Islamic state's history, see Braukamper 1977) it is extremely appropriate that Sheikh Husseen should have such significance as a contemporary symbol of Islamic identity. There is an interesting parallel here with Sheikh Aw Barkhadle, the most outstanding saint in northern Somalia (cf. above Ch. 7), who may likewise be regarded as representing the spiritual legacy of the Islamic state of Ifat-Adal, being indeed, as we have seen, one of the ancestors of the Walashma dynasty.

Although the cults of both saints may well contain a synthesis of pre-Islamic and Muslim cultural elements, this is more striking in the case of Sheikh Husseen than of Aw Barkhadle and reflects the more complex and heterogeneous ethnic history of   Bale in comparison with northern Somalia. Aw Barkhadle's shrine is essentially a Somali pilgrim centre. As Cerulli and others have so well demonstrated, the wide-ranging appeal of Sheikh Husseen's cult depends precisely on its syncretic character, blending Islamic elements with those from traditional Cushitic religion. This powerful combination of Oromo, Somali and Arab constituents gives Sheikh Husseen immense potency as a dynamic multifaceted symbol, a figure at once in the tradition of the Oromo divinely inspired *Qallus* and a Muslim saint through whose cult Islamic elements are readily absorbed. If this cult can thus in part be seen as the expression in religious form of currents of nascent Oromo nationalism, the ethnic identity that is projected has a strong Islamic tinge. Since the local Cushitic prototype of a Muslim has long been that of the Somali (cf. Baxter, 1966) – perhaps indeed for centuries – the effect is to enhance pan-Cushitic affinities with the Somali. (The custodians of Sheikh Husseen's tomb reportedly include Somalis). This seems a natural response to Christian Amhara domination, and to the failure of the old Amhara 'melting-pot' policy to fulfil the ethnic aspirations of the numerically dominant, but politically subordinate, Cushitic speakers.

SHEIKH HUSSEEN IN SOMALIA

Cerulli (1923 and 1938) and more recently Andrzejewski (1974-5) have drawn attention to the veneration accorded Sheikh Husseen in Somalia where, in the 1970s and 1980s, it was common to see mendicant friars whose Y-shaped walking-sticks and long rosaries announced their allegiance to the Sheikh. Sheikh Husseen also makes his presence felt by possessing women and recruiting them into special cult groups similar to those called *saar* in Somalia generally. The patient is treated by being smoked with incense, and made to eat roasted coffee beans (*bun*). The leaders of this cult which is also called 'Boranaa', have such Oromo names as Abba Sera (Father of Law), Abba Gada (Father of the Generation Sets), Hadda Sera (Mother of Law), etc. (Luling, 1977; Mohamed Abdi Mohamed, 1992). Through this possession cult, which seems very similar to that involving less specific 'holy spirits' called *wadaaddo* in northern Somalia (see Ch. 9), elements of Oromo culture in general, and Boranaa culture in particular, are diffused into southern Somali culture.

But the Somali connection with Sheikh Husseen extends far into the past behind these somewhat ambiguous contemporary manifestations. B. W. Andrzejewski (1975) has drawn attention to the genealogy linking Sheikh Husseen to contemporary descendants in

Merca on the Somali coast. Other genealogies which I collected in
Somalia in 1956 and 1962 near Bur Hacaba confirm this connection
(although they include a different number of generations). They
portray Sheikh Husseen as grandfather of the founder of a religious
lineage called the Walamogge, which figures prominently in the oral
traditions of southern Somalia. To this group, linked affinally with
the Ajuran, belong the Haran Madare.[2] The latter are widely
believed to have preceded the present Reer Sheikh Muumin (see
Ch.6) as guardians of the fertility of land and crops amongst the Elai
clan of Bur Hacaba. These traditions thus connect a former religious
dynasty (Haran Madare) amongst the Elai, with the Ajuran Sultanate (which in the 15th century dominated the lower Shabelle region)
and with Sheikh Husseen. As earlier writers have reported (e.g.
Bono, 1930), local traditions here have much to say of the part played
by the Haran Madare in overthrowing the tyrannical rule of the Ajuran Sultan's representative, Geedi Babo.

These intriguing connections between the history of this part of
southern Somalia and Sheikh Husseen in Bale receive further support from the fact that Bur Heibe, described to me in 1956 as the
'sacred mountain of the Rahanwiin', is the site of a complex of
shrines associated with Sheikh Husseen. Although not as elaborate
as its counterpart in Bale, the series of shrines and relics on the top of
Bur Heibe mountain[3] constitutes an important local centre of pilgrimage. Indeed, I was told that those who ascend the precipitate
mountain, and visit its shrines (not only for Sheikh Husseen, but also
for 'Abdul Qaadir al-Jiilani, 'Abul Qaasim, Asha, Faadumo (Fatima)
and Hawo) three times, acquire an amount of blessing equivalent to
that obtained by going once on pilgrimage to Mecca. Thus this pilgrimage complex of Sheikh Husseen shrines in southern Somalia
has the same mystical value as that of Sayyid Aw Barkhadle in
Somaliland – a further point of resemblance between the two great
saints.

MODERN OROMO AND SOMALI ETHNICITY

This parallelism extends to the two saints' connections with histori-
cally important Muslim states in the Horn of Africa (Ifat and Bale). If
Aw Barkhadle binds northern Somalia to a Muslim past centring on
Zeila and Harar and embracing related Cushitic-speaking people
(Afar and Beja), Sheikh Husseen's twin pilgrimage centres in Bale
and Bur Hacaba commemorate similar relations in south-eastern
Ethiopia. This mystically charged Cushitic cultural capital,
enhanced by many generations of accrued interest, provided high-

yielding assets in the portfolio of the WSLF freedom fighters. But there remains a key issue which has still to be faced. If those Arusi, Boranaa and other Oromo who embrace Islam assume the ethnic identity of Somali, what is the fate of those – and they are almost certainly the majority of Oromo – who remain? How far into Oromo ethnicity can an Oromo-Somali identity be extended? What are its limits and how, if the WSLF were to succeed in its aims, would the aspirations of the remaining Oromo be accommodated? Some indication of the problems and tensions involved here is provided by the angry rejection by certain Muslim Oromo nationalists – who are as opposed to Amhara domination as anyone – of the Somali-biased designation 'Somali Abo', despite the formation in 1976 of the Bali-based Somali-Abo Liberation Front (SALF) as a collateral movement allied to the WSLF. Oromo groups were clearly distancing themselves from Somali, a process further encouraged by the politics of regionalism in the explicitly pluralist polity of 1990s Ethiopia.

Notes

1   This represents an interesting reversal of the earlier trend of 'Oromisation' in Bale where it is customary to distinguish between 'true' Oromo (*Humbanu*) and assimilated Somali, Harari and others, known as *(Sarri)* Sidama (see Braukamper, 1977). In this area, at any rate, ethnicity is very permeable, and its contours flow back and forth according to circumstances. Somalis can become Oromos, just as Oromo can become Somali. Indeed many sections of the Ajuran and Garre clans in north-eastern Kenya, known formerly as 'half-Somali', are bilingual in Somali and Oromo. These clans represent a fluid half-way house between the two ethnic groups and are the most direct link between Somali 'Abo' and Somali 'Wariiya'.

2   According to some sources, the Haran Madare Walamogge are direct lineal descendants (rather than affines) of the Ajuran.

3   A tradition, which I recorded at Bur Hacaba in 1962, attributes the formation of the group of three mountains (Bur Hacaba, Bur Heibe and Bur Heleda) to which Bur Heibe belongs, to the miraculous power of Sheikh Husseen. This story recounts how Sheikh Husseen was one day sitting in Arabia with the great saint, 'Abdul Qaadir al-Jiilani, when the latter challenged him to display his powers by taking up a local mountain and casting it across the sea. Husseen Baliale, so the tale maintains, threw the mountain into southern Somalia where it broke into three separate pieces, one becoming Bur Hacaba, one Bur Heibe and the third Bur Heleda. Inside the miraculous mountain was 'Abdul Qaasim who is accordingly venerated at Bur Heibe.

Chapter 9

UNRULY SPIRITS: A CHALLENGE TO ISLAM?

As Muslims participating in the world culture of Islam, the Somali lack much of that immediacy in the mystical evaluation of human affairs which is so characteristic of many tribal religious systems. This is partly explicable in terms of orthodox Muslim eschatology, according to which, as Somali believe, the final evaluation of man's conduct is not experienced in this life but in the hereafter. Thus the unjust and those whose religious observance and moral conduct leave much to be desired may enjoy greater worldly fortunes and success than those who scrupulously honour the tenets of their faith. Only on the day of reckoning will the account be finally settled and the righteous rewarded for their devotion and effort. This separation between the mundane social order and divine retribution is, I believe, further strengthened by the ease with which so many conflicts are resolved by a direct appeal to physical force. Petty disputes are readily blown up into serious issues involving large numbers of people, and feud and fighting are widespread and frequent.

Nevertheless, although God's ultimate judgement will only be revealed and experienced in the after-life, God is regularly approached in prayer and sacrifice, through the mediation of the Prophet Mahammad, to intervene in human suffering. Indeed, men turn equally to Him in despair and thanksgiving. And since Somali hold that man is inherently sinful and far removed from God's grace, powerful advocates are needed to plead with God through the Prophet if their prayers are to be answered. Here men turn for help to those holymen (sing. *wadaad*) and saints (sing. *weli*) whose religious devotion to God has been rewarded by enabling them to perform miraculous works. As we have seen, it is through the blessing (*baraka*) of these saints particularly – and this includes all lineage ancestors as well as men remembered for their personal piety – that the Prophet is petitioned to intercede with God.

Living holymen and saints are, as emphasised in previous chapters, ideally excluded from full participation in the secular warrior life of Somali pastoral society. Their role is that of non-combatant mediators, and their mystical influence which includes the power of applying the curse (*habaar*) or sorcery (*sihir*) to uphold their authority appears as, in effect, a compensation for their lack of direct secular power. It is possible indeed to discern a well-defined polarity in Somali notions of power such that those who lack secular strength – either in general, or sometimes only in special situations – are considered to be correspondingly mystically endowed (cf. Lewis, 1963). This mystical coverage is extended to include destitute old women whom it is dangerous to treat with contempt and rewarding to treat with kindness; and the position is much the same with such traditionally despised minority communities of craftsmen as the Yibir soothsayers who wander from camp to camp. There is thus a fairly wide spectrum of categories of persons who, while of very different social status, and lacking effective secular force, at least in certain situations share the property of mystical power. At one end of the scale are those such as saints, whose special mystical powers unequivocally emanate directly from God; at the other pole there are those, such as the Yibirs, whose mystical force derives from sources which are closely connected with the devil (*shaydaan*).

Spirit-possession is also associated with the devil, or with devils, and in this chapter I shall argue that this phenomenon is invoked to account for physical and mental distress (rather than misfortune) in situations where those afflicted are in some sense deprived of secular efficacy. I shall also argue that spirit-possession, in this cultural context, is closely associated with gender and with relations between the sexes. Persons who thus lack power, deprived are not sources of mystical danger to others so much as themselves endangered, and it is only in the institutionalized means of treatment for spirit-possession afflictions that the victims obtain a measure of redress, and thus obliquely put pressure on others. My argument here is thus that, in conformity with the general notions outlined above, spirit-possession, diagnosed in cases of mental and physical disturbance, is a refuge of the weak and injured: it is utilized by those who seek redress but find other means of effective action blocked or culturally inappropriate. Again, it has to be emphasised that to a variable extent, those concerned are not necessarily weak and helpless in a total sense, but sometimes only in a particular context.

Along with cursing, sorcery, and the evil eye, spirit-possession thus features as one explanation of physical and mental distress. But all sickness is not explained in such terms. Like health and good fortune, illness generally is ultimately in God's power to withhold or bestow, and in my experience it is usually in such fatalistic terms that most afflictions are accepted and endured. The afflicted seek relief through prayers and offerings to God, while Muslim prophylactics are freely employed, and full use is made of such resources of modern medical treatment as may be available. It should be added that, as well as some expertise in bone-setting and such surgical operations as tripanning,[1] Somalis possess a considerable diagnostic medical lore,[2] including knowledge (before this was generally know to the Western scientific world) of the carrying of malaria by mosquitoes. However, the therapeutic value of traditional pharmaceutical and other treatment (cupping, blood-letting, and cauterization) can scarcely have been great.[3]

In interpreting and treating sickness, consequently, it is the context of its occurrence, rather than its actual physical symptoms that decide which cause is sought and accepted and what treatment is followed. And as will be seen, there is often dispute as to the cause of illness. Spirit-possession, or 'entering' as it is generally described, figures as such a cause only in a limited and fairly clearly defined range of contexts. In my experience, four such contexts can be distinguished where 'illness' is ascribed to possession, and these I follow here. The symptoms, it may be as well to add at this stage, include such diverse elements as fainting, falling down, vomiting, feebleness, bodily aches and pains, and general malaise and depression, as well as such classical features as violent bodily agitation and epilepsy. Madness, also, is often (but not invariably) attributed to spirit possession. Of the four contexts which I recorded and examine here, the first concerns the possesson of a man by a woman he has jilted, or by a woman whom he desires but cannot marry. The second is concerned with the possession of young camel-herders in circumstances of deprivation and sexual frustration. The third involves the possession of married women when they experience hardship and frustration. The fourth concerns men, again generally in circumstances of personal affliction and distress. It is thus not merely illness as such which invokes spirit-possession as its cause, but illness, real or imagined, in these contexts.

In the first case there is a direct and obvious nexus of personal feeling (as with the contexts in which the 'evil eye' is thought to operate) and the person possessed is said to be 'entered' by the person he has thwarted, or who is the cause of his frustration. In the other three contexts this nexus is less obvious or clearly defined, and is less directly referred to, since the possessed person's affliction is not directly related to the human source of antagonism and injury but treated obliquely as a sickness caused by a spirit. And consistently with this indirect relationship between the victim and the source of antagonism, the spirit involved here is not, as in the first case, that of a person, but a nature sprite belonging to that mysterious host of mischievous powers which as Muslims the Somali know under the generic name of jinns.

These spirits, which are anthropomorphic in character, being said to be 'just like people', are thought to frequent deserted houses, and old camp sites, caves, forests, particular trees and all dark, empty places. During the day, particularly, they live in the shade, often underground, but appear at night and can sometimes be seen by man. The form they then assume may be no more substantial than that of a will-o'-the-wisp. Uncanny and mysterious appearances of light at night may be attributed to them, and a shooting star is pictur-esquely said to be one struck down by an angel. Like people, they own livestock, live in their own houses, marry, and engage in trade and commerce and have their own shops and markets. Like man-kind too, as Somalis know from their own experience of society, some are learned in the Koran and may quote back chapter and verse of the sacred book when passages of the Koran are invoked against them. Some, following orthodox Muslim theology, are regarded as believers.

These sprites are particularly closely connected in Somali thought with wild animals. Thus they need no zaribas to defend their flock from attack from wild animals as men do, for all the wild animals are their friends. The hyena, which owing to the anatomical peculiari-ties of its genital organs Somalis regard as a hermaphrodite, and which takes a considerable toll of livestock as well as sometimes attacking the unwary shepherd as he sleeps at night, is considered to be particularly closely connected with jinns. Some indeed say that it is a jinn; moreover, a species of large lizard (maso'agalay), and a smaller fat-tailed lizard, both harmless to man, should not be killed since they are believed to be the 'wives' of jinns.

These devils, as they are often described by Somali, are essentially malign and dangerous to man. Although some are Muslims, they stand opposed to God and seek to subvert his moral order: yet ulti-mately God is believed to have control over them, as over every other creature. These contradictions, which to some extent reflect the ambiguous character of the divinity as at once the source of blessing and of suffering, are evident in conflicting opinions as to the power directing jinns when they molest man. Of those which are considered to be Muslims and learned and which I refer to as 'learned sprites' (*wadaaddo*)[4], it is sometimes said that they are sent by God, though this is by no means the generally accepted view. Despite these obscurities and ambiguities concerning their relationship to God, their most general attribution is to the Devil and they are seen as his agents or 'soldiers', parallel with the ranks of angels who support and execute the commands of God. As there is a struggle within men between right and wrong, good or bad, so the forces of light and those of darkness are similarly pictured as locked in continuous conflict. These sprites consequently become endowed with the envy and covetousness, and the corresponding malice, which are part of human experience and of which they serve as objectifications. It is believed that there are men who are also jinns, and that these may unleash their devils on those they envy. Envy and desire are likewise held to provide the animus for the generality of these demons which have no human familiars to enter and trouble men. No living thing except the date-palm is immune from their unwelcome attentions.

Since they lurk everywhere, care must always be taken lest these malignant sprites enter a person's body and harm him. Plates and dishes containing food are covered at night to prevent jinns getting into them and so entering the body; and milking vessels are treated on the inside with smoke from burning incense, not merely to make the milk especially palatable and waterproof the container, but also to protect it from contamination. Incense, which is invested with religious power, and the leaves and barks of all pleasantly smelling trees and plants, are regarded as affording protection against these noxious powers, and employed in exorcising them. Thus, on all occasions when the presence of jinns is feared, men burn incense to drive them away; and at dusk as men gather round the fires in the camps it is usual to sprinkle a little incense among the flames with the pious words: 'God deliver us from the devils, In the name of God, the Compassionate, the Merciful'.

It is important to emphasize that although certain individuals are believed to have an 'agreement' with a jinn, these sprites are essentially free-ranging and autonomous, they are not regularly linked to individuals or to groups; and the only respect in which they can be said to 'mirror' the social structure is in their division into the unlearned and learned, parallelling the division of human society between those who are warriors (*waranleh*) and those who are holymen of God (*wadaads*). There is no conception of their being grouped in descent groups corresponding to the basic social divisions of society. They are believed, moreover, to behave entirely arbitrarily and capriciously, and there is no connection between them and the souls of the dead, or the ancestors of either individuals or groups. Thus the relationship which Firth has cautiously noted between social structure and spirit hierarchy in his comparison of Tikopia and Malay spirit beliefs, is not found here (see Firth, 1959, 142).

Spirit-possession for Somali is essentially an illness, an unwanted, undesirable state associated with affliction and suffering: spirits cause disease, they do not cure it. To understand how the four contexts – in which illness is so ascribed to possession – relate directly to personal powerlessness, we have to consider briefly some of the salient aspects of Somali social structure, particularly those concerning the position of women and the character of the traditional etiquette governing relations between the sexes.

THE ROLES OF MEN AND WOMEN IN TRADITIONAL PASTORAL SOCIETY

In a fluid setting of frequent movement from pasture to pasture where ties to locality count for little, social relations are primarily based upon agnatic descent. In day-to-day affairs, as we have seen, people's loyalties are more narrowly circumscribed by their membership of small contractually defined lineage groups whose members in concert pay and receive blood-compensation for injury and death. These groups are rapidly mobilized in the disputes and feuds in which Somali are so regularly embroiled through the incessant friction which prevails over access to the sparse water and grazing resources of their country.[5]

Although their members are often scattered geographically, and they are not thus strictly localized, these units are clearly defined groups and normally marriage within them is forbidden by strong and explicit legal sanctions. Women pass physically at marriage from the *dia*-paying responsibility of their father to that of their husband, in return for the receipt of considerable marriage payments. Yet, although a wife is subject to the authority of her husband, she continues to retain strong jural ties with her own natal *dia*-paying group (maintaining her own natal identity); and it is they rather than the husband and his agnates who bear the brunt of responsibility in paying or receiving blood-money incurred in respect of her life. Thus, if a man's wife is murdered, he has no full title to her blood-wealth, but only a claim to a sororatic replacement from her kin (cf. Lewis, 1962).

Whether as daughters or as wives, women are subject to strong and direct jural control by their menfolk. A man may, within limits that are only vaguely defined, beat an erring wife and can expect the support of her kin in any corrective action he takes as long as they are interested in the maintenance of the marriage. Indeed, the perfect image of the husband, as of the father, is the stern *pater familias* with full authority to compel obedience and submission. On his wedding night, according to tradition, the husband is expected to chastise his wife with a small ceremonial whip, the public display of which is a sign of his newly married position. These powers vested in men are firmly upheld by the Muslim legal courts, although a woman can, at least in theory, appeal against excessive physical mistreatment. Husbands, moreover, can divorce their wives very easily, and in fact do, while women cannot directly gain divorce and can only have their marriages annulled, on such grounds as the physical incapacity of their husband, on recourse to a Muslim court. They can of course resort to other remedies – such as simply absconding. But as long as the wife's kin are committed to the continuance of her marriage every effort will be made by them to find the run-away wife, and, if caught, she will be beaten and returned to her husband. In the end, however, such desperate tactics, when repeated sufficiently often, are likely to force even the most reluctant of husbands to concede divorce. Yet the position nevertheless remains, that society greatly strengthens the husband's hand and weakens that of the wife. So that even where a wife does thus force divorce upon her husband, she is likely to forfeit the Islamic personal dower which her husband undertook to give her when he married her, and to which she is entitled on termination of her marriage.

Throughout their lives women remain, in effect, second-class citizens. A woman's blood-wealth is generally rated as half that of a man (i.e. fifty instead of one hundred camels), and women's rights to inherit property under Islamic law are rarely fully honoured, particularly where such capital assets as camels are concerned. The obverse of these disabilities is that in all public transactions a women has the right to call upon the support and help of her menfolk. It is their duty to supply her with adequate subsistence, to protect her interests generally, and to carry out all those tasks which it is unseemly for a woman directly to execute herself. Women, like young children, are conceived traditionally as being weak and defenceless and ideally they should provide a submissive and passive foil to the aggressive dominance and masculinity of their husbands and male kin. A woman who displays independent initiative, courage and fortitude will be described with grudging praise as a 'man'; while on other occasions men will readily complain how feeble, demanding and unreliable their womenfolk are.

In the same vein, a man should ideally be complete and self-reliant, and it is unmanly and dishonourable, traditionally, for men to display open affection for their wives. Men should address their wives brusquely, and the latter reply in an appropriate submissive tone, at least in public. At the level of actual behaviour as distinct from ideals of conduct between the sexes, the exigencies of the nomadic life demand that men must be ready to leave their wives and homes at a moment's notice to see to the needs of their herds in distant pastures, to join in their watering at the wells, or to engage in other activities connected with clan politics or trade which may take them away from home for unspecified periods. No man whose conduct reveals that he is emotionally dependent upon his wife, or wives, can hope to enjoy a reputation for male hardihood. Indeed, those who betray such a lack of independence are unfailingly stigmatized as being little better than women. In the same tight-lipped puritanical tradition, the ideal of pre-marital chastity in women is strongly held, and the practice of female infibulation is seen as a device to ensure virginity at marriage. Traditionally, there is very little open courting prior to matrimony and arranged matches are common. Only engaged couples are sometimes allowed some degree of licence to indulge to a limited degree in sexual play.

Young men are, in any case, by the nature of their herding duties with the camels, removed for weeks and sometimes months on end from contact with the girls who look after the sheep and goats in the camps. The camps, composed of the wives and children of closely related men (often brothers), who themselves are often away, and the flocks of sheep and goats upon which they depend for subsistence, move largely independently of the grazing camels in the charge of young herders. The camels are far more mobile and wide-ranging in their movements than the flocks which are so much more demanding in their water requirements. The former, consequently, can be taken out to areas of lush pasture far from the families and sheep and goats which, in the dry seasons especially, have always to keep close to the wells. These two herding units, the one in the care of boys and unmarried men, and the other in the charge of women and marriageable girls and young children, tend to move closer, or to camp together, after the rains when there is plenty of fresh pasture. It is in this season that the young camel-herders have an opportunity of contact with girls of marriageable age and there is a general expansion in the range and intensity of social life.

From an early age the distinction and separation of the sexes are stressed. Girls, who wear clothing which always discreetly conceals their pudenda, are taught to look after the sheep and goats, to milk them, and to weave ropes and cords from bark fibre. At the same time, they help in the preparation and cooking of food and the care of their younger siblings. Boys, who are often less modestly clothed, also help with the management of the sheep and goats until the age of about seven when they are sent out with their elder brothers and cousins to learn the rudiments of camel husbandry. This involves them in long and lonely treks with the camels and introduces them to a hard and exacting life in which they enjoy few comforts. Normally they have no cooking utensils with them and have to subsist on the milk of the camels in their charge. In the dry seasons particularly, when milk is scarce and there is little water to satisfy their thirst, their lot is not an enviable one. This is the severe training school in which they learn to endure the rigours of hunger and thirst and to cultivate those attitudes of alertness and suspicion that are so strongly engrained in the Somali character.

After marriage, men spend less time out with the camels, except when they lack younger agnatic kin, or servants, to supervise their herds (and flocks), and play an important part in regulating watering movements and in preparing the wells which often have to be dug out seasonally. Their other main task and interests lie in the field of clan politics: and they are often away from their tents and wives, pursuing these interests, visiting their herds, or making expeditions to trading centres to buy provisions. Married women are less mobile. Though they may take milk or clarified butter to sell in neighbouring markets, and also lead caravans of camels to the wells to bring back drinking water for the household, they play an essentially domestic role concerned with child caring and cooking. They are associated only with the burden camels which they load with their collapsible huts or tents and all their effects when they move camp. The milking camels are the concern of men, and only men milk them.

The differentiating effects of this sexual divison of labour are reinforced by a partial application of Muslim notions of purdah. Women, amongst the nomads, are not veiled or strictly secluded; but the woman's part of the tent may not be entered by men other than her husband or kin, except at the risk of incurring charges of adultery. Women, likewise, eat separately from their menfolk. The head of the family and his guests are served first, while women eat afterwords with the children.

This almost total domestic involvement of women, in contrast to the men's monopoly of public affairs, is also strongly emphasised in religious worship. Although, like men, women are frequent visitors at the shrines of saints to which they go to seek relief from affliction as well as in search of fecundity, they are almost totally excluded from full participation in the public Muslim cult. They are not admitted to the mosques where men regularly pray; they do not participate effectively in the highly developed activities and regular ceremonies of the mystical religious orders or 'brotherhoods' which play such a vital part in men's religious life; and at large-scale public Muslim feasts and festivals they gather only on the periphery of the all-male crowd, trilling at appropriate points in the rites. While a considerable number of men succeed in going on pilgrimage to Mecca, few women accomplish this highly prestige-giving act of devotion. Thus, in religious life also, women play an essentially passive role. They are not expected to be ostensibly devout, as men are, and the fact that they rarely observe the obligatory daily prayers excites little adverse comment. In sum, it is not going too far, I think, to suggest that men consider that their own active public devotion is sufficient to excuse the relatively passive religiosity of their womenfolk. It is this background of confinement and constriction in the relations between the sexes, and in the overall position of women, which illuminates most of the contexts in which spirit-possession occurs amongst the northern Somali. There is one striking exception with which we deal first.

YOUNG MEN'S POSSESSION

The most general term in Somali for possession by a spirit is *gelid*, meaning literally 'entering' (from the verb *gal*, to enter), and the victim is said to have 'caught' (*qab*)[6] the spirit in the same way that other illnesses and diseases are 'caught', and to be in turn held in its thrall to the extent that he speaks with its voice, and voices its demands. The victim is also described as having 'yielded', 'succumbed' or 'agreed' to the spirit, so that the notions involved, at least grammatically, include participation and implied compliance on the part of the victim as well as of the invading spirit. The accompanying physical symptoms, ranging from mild hysteria to acute physical symptons, are very varied, as we have seen.

The most personalized and varied notions of spirit-possession come into play when a young man exhibits any or all of these symptoms in what we would describe, in a western context, as that of unrequited or frustrated love. The standard situation here is where the youth has jilted a girl. A man may, for example, be troubled by a girl who loves him and whom he promised to marry but did not. If a young man falls sick in these circumstances, it is suspected that the girl who desires him and whom he has abandoned has possessed him. She will not let him go. The actual agency and mechanism by which this form of possession occurs is not explained very precisely. The girl is said simply to have 'entered' the man. It is obvious that this statement is intended to be understood in a metaphorical rather than a literal sense, and further enquiry reveals that Somalis are not much concerned by their difficulties in explaining the process which occurs. If pressed, however, it will be suggested that the girl has sent a jinn to trouble the man[7]. This, indeed, is the only explanation Somalis can offer since any suggestion that the girl's soul (*naf*) is the agency of possession is excluded. The soul, the immortal essence of a person, leaves the human body only at death, which it survives as the sensate entity to experience God's rewards and punishments.

Here, as in other cases of possession, the standard treatment consists in the exorcism of the invading agency. This is administered by a holyman who intones passages from the Koran (particularly the sixty-sixth Sura, known as *Yaasiin*) against the spirit while the victim is shrouded in blankets, and incense is burned on a fire, producing dense choking fumes. This atmosphere is, of course, well calculated to stimulate dissociation in the patient, but I am doubtful if dissociation actually occurs in the majority of cases. Whether it does or not, however, the patient is well prepared from his own cultural training to make the stock responses which the situation requires.

At the beginning of the treatment, the invading spirit identifies herself according to the following formula: 'I am a girl named..., and I desire this man. He promised to marry me, but did not'. As the treatment proceeds, the spirit is alternately cajoled and threatened by the might of God's word to quit its victim, the cleric conducting the treatment incessantly muttering, 'If you don't come out, I will burn you'. Burning here refers to the fiery power of the verses from the Koran and the cleansing efficacy of the smouldering incense. The spirit, in successful treatments, responds to these threats by a series of stereotyped formulae indicating the line of its retreat. It promises to withdraw from the body of the victim through his chin, through his nose, his ears, and other points on his frame. But not until the spirit says that it is coming out by 'the little finger of the left hand' is the exorcism considered complete and the patient discharged as cured. As far as I am aware, this stereotyped phrase is not used in other contexts, but for the Somali, as for other Muslims, the left hand is inauspicious, almost unclean; and the little finger is regarded as weak and puny and as the least useful of the fingers.

Skeptical observers who are not intimately concerned for the well-being of the victim point out that in seances of this kind the voice of the 'spirit' is identical to that of its host. Those directly involved view the matter differently. In one instance which I heard of but did not witness, a holyman was said to have attributed the death of a wife and daughter to this type of possession. When he later married another woman she in turn fell sick, experiencing fainting fits in which she uttered the name of another woman. This woman, whom his wife knew to covet her husband, was diagnosed as the cause of the malady, and the man was advised to sacrifice a ram and to offer its blood to appease the spirit. When this was drunk by his sick wife (being consumed by the invading spirit) she gradually recovered; or so I was told.

What is clear in such cases is the basis of personal antagonism, directing the attack of the invading spirit, and generally stemming from unrequited love between men and women. That frustrated desire should find expression in this pattern of mystical retaliation is consistent with the fact that in situations of this kind no formal legal redress is possible for the woman. Breach of promise between private individuals is not a recognised tort, and it is only when a formal engagement exists and preliminary marriage payments have been made that court proceedings can be pursued involving not merely the individuals directly concerned, but also their kinsmen. Private understandings, where they exist, cannot be subject to litigation, and passionate feelings between the sexes cannot traditionally be directly vented in public.

Where young men's desires are frustrated the position is very similar since, as we have seen, for a man to express openly any attachment to a woman is shameful in the extreme. It is perfectly understandable that the same malady is sometimes diagnosed in the case of a man who falls sick when he is prevented, by the opposition of his father and elder kinsmen, from marrying the girl of his choice. For, a man who rejects the noble expedient of elopement and accepts the decision of his elders must conceal his feelings. Whilst possession of a man by a woman in these circumstances is seen by young educated Somalis today very much as we would see it – as simply a case of disappointed love where the idea of a love-match simply could not be entertained – spirit-possession provided the only acceptable idiom in which such instances of frustrated desire could be presented without shame. Illness brings no dishonour.

This line of interpretation applies equally to a kindred type of possession, which often manifests itself in young camel-herders when they return from their hard life of solitude and isolation, to the warmth and excitement of the family camps and the girls who await them there. On these occasions some herders often evince signs of hysteria which are interpreted as a form of spirit-possession. The smitten youths are not considered to be suffering from an illness, but rather to be temporarily mentally disturbed, being described as 'mad', a word which in Somali as in English connotes many degrees of perturbation, ranging from wrath to extreme insanity. Here it is not the spirit of a particular person which causes this state, but a nature sprite called *saar*, this term denoting both the spirit and the condition of the person possessed. The word *saar* calls for some explanation in view of its connection with the Ethiopian shamanistic *zar* cult, but I defer this to a later section, merely noting here that whatever its origin, *saar* has peculiar semantic appropriateness, since in other contexts it signifies something that is placed on top of something else (for example, a parasitic creeper), and is also used to describe the position of the adopted stranger client – one who comes inside from without.

When a youth in these circumstances becomes hysterical, his companions mount a dance, known as 'beating the sprite', for his relief. The intention is clearly and explicitly cathartic, and it is essential that girls should participate in the dance if it is to be effective. The dancers form a loose circle round the possessed boy, and begin dancing slowly, to the accompaniment of hand-clapping and the singing of a standardized chorus, an example of which I give below. The tempo mounts and the afflicted youth begins gyrating in the centre of the circle, his movements becoming wilder and wilder as he sings his solo song, again of a standardized form, commanding general attention, and then breaking into a song – composed for the occasion – in which he announces his plight. This of course is said to be the sprite singing in him; and, as the tension mounts, the youth frequently seizes a stick or sword, threatening those gathered round him with hysterical and exaggerated gestures. As he does this, with, at any rate on the few occasions when I have witnessed the scene, a truly frenzied expression, the sprite possessing him shouts 'Catch me; do not catch me' as he darts towards and then away from his companions. At last, after a short space of time which may be no more than an hour, he drops sweating and exhausted on the ground, apparently in a trance-like state. From this, he eventually rises muttering the Muslim creed: 'There is no God but Allah, and Mahammad is His Prophet', and recovers his normal state. The explicit significance of this gesture is that he was alienated from normal human society and from God and has now returned to his senses and to Islam. Also explicit is the notion of the opposition between God and his works, and the capricious and malevolent world of jinn, noted earlier.

The introductory chorus, sung as the party begins to 'beat the *saar*' takes the following form:

The spirit and the seas have grown small [?receded]
La, La, La...
You don't invite the devil.
Take shelter from it by reciting 'In the name of God,
The Compassionate, the Merciful',

Then the smitten boy commands attention with some such lines as:

All you saints and men of God,
All you white-haired boys[8]
And all you women,
Until I say the word
Keep your mouths shut for me!

This is repeated three times, and then the youth sings his own or some other *saar* sprite song describing his condition. Four typical examples are the following:

i.   Like the winged hornbill in flight
      I am herded with the stars,
      I drink from the rain-shower as it falls from heaven.
      I don't accept cool clapping,
      Loud and rumbustious is the rhythm I know
      I drink blood
      Then I recover my senses.

In the following song, the singer is less concerned with his own state of alienation and exhaltation, and refers more directly to the intention of the dance:

ii.   Oh girls, abuse and praise
      Are stored in my stomach.
      Which do you prefer?
      Which shall I spread my blanket for?

In the next song the singer announces his complete dedication to the *saar*:

iii. Birds flock in trees
      Each has its own call
      No one understands the others.
      Let the administrative officer imprison me for years on end
      Let him cut off my nose and ears
      Let him force me to give up my religion
      Let him chain my legs.
      Whatever I suffer, I will never give up the *saar*.

In the final example, the possessed youth simply boasts of the superiority of his own kinsmen's interpretation of this dance:

iv.   Did I not tell you so, Oh Rubo? [a girl's name]
     Apart from our own people, Oh Rubo,
     All other people,
     The way they beat the *saar*
     Is unaccomplished.

In the puritanical traditional ethic of the pastoralists which condemns overt courting and discourages mixed dancing, this context of possession is little more than a special type of dance which permits and encourages men to give vent to erotic feelings in a culturally acceptable mode. For the camel-herders returned from their world of isolation and hardship, it represents a welcome release and indeed a sublimation, since there is no question of the *saar* dancers indulging in actual sexual intercourse. Yet the erotic intention is almost explicit in many of the songs sung on these occasions, and it is significant that the phrase 'to beat the *saar*' is also a colloquialism for sexual intercourse.

Thus this dance is characterized as a form of play (*ayar*) or game, rather than as a serious ritual designed to remove illness, although it is recognized that certain youths are more than usually prone to this type of hysteria and may, when so possessed, be a danger to themselves and others.[9] It is also recognized that in many cases a boy may sham possession in order to have the opportunity of displaying his desire, through this dance, for a particular girl, or that he may adopt this device to attract the attention of a girl he loves and to impress her with the strength of his desire. Today, with the growth of more liberal attitudes towards relations between the sexes, the dance seems increasingly to have these latter functions, particularly where it is performed in towns. It has also been adopted under the name of *baahilaawe* or *baar'adde* in certain rituals associated with the ceremonies performed in honour of a number of local saints, particularly in that connected with the cult of Sheikh Husseen Baliale, whose tomb in southern Ethiopia, as we have seen, is one of the most widely frequented shrines in north-east Africa. It has thus found a precarious niche in the general cult of saints, but one which orthodox holymen regard as heterodox, and the ceremonies of which it forms part were consequently officially banned in the former Somali Republic.

WOMEN'S POSSESSION AFFLICTIONS

By far the most common form of possession in Somaliland is that afflicting women and generally attributed to the malign influence of the same category of sprites as the preceding *saar* type. Here, however, possession is regarded (especially by women) as a disease which is often serious. A number of distinct, named *saar* sprites are recognised as the agents responsible (I noted a dozen such individually named demons), and treatment, which is costly though often only temporarily successful, is always by a woman specialist or shaman (*alaaqad*) who is described as having 'authority' over the sprites. Such experts are almost invariably widows, childless women, or divorcees, and not infrequently managers of brothels or dens where men can meet to chew the stimulant leaves of the *qat* plant, the succulent leaves of which contain drugs of the benzedrine family). All are women who have in the past been, or are recurrently subject to *saar* possession and who generally fail in some important respects to conform to the ideal of Somali womanhood which is that of the dutiful married woman with children.

Those mediums who are most widely respected claim to have been initiated into the appropriate propitiation mysteries and to have secured authority to conduct their seances from similar experts in Ethiopia, where the *saar* (*zar*) cult is highly developed among Christians, Muslims and others (see Leiris, 1958, Messing, 1958; Lewis, 1989 passim). In keeping with this association, the most serious sprite afflictions are often ascribed to 'Ethiopian sprites' (*saar habashi*, also known as *menghis*), and in the prevailing context of Somali-Ethiopian animosity (in the 1950s and 1960s), this was sometimes explained by Somali as a kind of retaliatory mystical scourge sent against them by the Ethiopians. Although the actual date of the introduction of the belief in these *saar* sprites is unknown, there is, I think, little doubt as to its ultimate origin in Ethiopia, whence the belief has also spread to Arabia, northern Sudan and Egypt (see Cerulli, 1936; and for *zar* in Khartoum, Barclay, 1964, 196-209; Boddy, 1990; Lewis, al-Safi, Hurreiz, eds.1991). This, however, is not to say that the Somali interpretation of the *zar* complex contains all the elements found in Ethiopia or in these other countries into which it has spread. The emphasis in Somaliland is, as I have said, on exorcism[*], rather than on shamanism as it operates in Ethiopia. Nor does the cult as it functions here – unlike in Ethiopia and in Khartoum – provide an actual corporate organisation through which the members of depressed classes can

---

[*] Or so I first thought; further consideration has caused me to move towards regarding *saar* possession as a form of shamanism. (See Lewis, 1989.)

enhance their security and status. Thus the Somali mediums normally claim no particular gifts as seers or fortune-tellers and have no special standing in contexts other than the treatment of the afflicted.

Treatment, conducted by the medium, ranges from elaborate seances akin to those regularly practised in Ethiopia, to simpler ceremonies involving only the patient and her doctor. Whatever the form of therapy, the medium is handsomely rewarded for her services and the essence of treatment consists in the appeasement of the possessing sprite by the presentation of luxurious gifts to the patient. These, paid for by the patient's husband or other relatives, include such acceptable articles as perfume, silks, other clothes and finery, as well as such especially delectable foods as sweetmeats, dates, coffee and tea. This theme of luxurious presents and sociability, contrasting sharply with the rigours of the nomadic life, is strongly emphasized.

The *saar* sprites are always described as liking and coveting 'all good things', all the things in fact that every Somali wife hankers after; and there is an ambivalent aspect since the sprite may attack a woman when she is got up in all her finery, and consequently is sensitive to the envy of others, as much as when she herself is reduced to wearing rags and envies other better-dressed women.

Thus a woman described how she had first become possessed many years before:

> I was staying at Berbera, and one dark night, wearing good clothes, I walked along a deserted alley between two houses. Finally something caught me and flung me to the ground. I was carried home and found that I had broken out in boils. That is because I had walked over a sprite which bit me and caused me to fall ill. The *saar* sprite attacked me because I was wearing good clothes and perfume. I was ill for three days and then cured by a medium. I was afflicted by an Ethiopian sprite called 'Mamme'. Sometimes when I'm not wearing good clothes the sprite still beats me.

The ambiguity herein provides an effective rationale for the commonly expressed women's view that these sprites attack both the rich and the poor and that no woman is immune from them. Sometimes this is stated more precisely, women maintaining that certain specific sprites attack only the poor, while others confine their attentions to the well-to-do.

In the most elaborate cathartic seances (which I have not myself seen, men being rigorously excluded) the spirit medium is said to wear black clothes while her female attendants are dressed in red and the patient herself is clad in her oldest clothes. When cured at the end of the rite she is expected to put on red clothing. These sprites are definitely connected symbolically with the colour red and are sometimes identified with a 'red wind'; they are also said to take a person's blood, and the offering of blood to them is an important element in many of the cathartic rites.

In the seance, the afflicted woman may be placed on top of an ox while the other women sing *saar* songs conjuring up the sprite, or 'beating the *saar*' as it is again described, and rousing the patient to a pitch of hysterical frenzy as in the camel-herder's dance. Drums or paraffin tins are beaten in an increasingly fast tempo, and the women attendants uncover and dishevel their hair in various gestures of abandonment. (Married women normally wear their hair modestly hidden beneath a black handkerchief.) The presiding medium stands in the centre, often wielding a sword, while the victim is led round on the ox's back wriggling her body and shoulders in time with the rhythm. After some time, the subject of the rite falls swooning on the ground, the dance is stopped, and the ox is killed. When the patient recovers, she is helped upright and steps over the ox's blood. The medium and the acolytes and the patient and her women friends then cook and eat the meat of the slaughtered beast. All the expense incurred and the medium's fee are borne by the patient. In the less elaborate ceremonies which are more commonly held, a cock, sheep or goat is killed for the sprite, and the party feasts on this meat and boiled rice or grain. Tea and coffee are also prepared and dates and other delicacies are passed round, and perfume (as in a religious ceremony involving men) is liberally sprinkled on the participants.

No matter how simple the ceremony, the 'exorcism' always entails considerable expense. Generous amounts of food and other luxury articles are required 'for the sprite' (i.e. for the patient) and for the medium who administers the treatment. One man claimed, for instance, that in addition to the medium's cash for the treatment of his wife, the latter had been instructed to buy four large bottles of perfume, twenty pounds of dates, and ample quantities of sugar, grain, tea, garlic, onions, and potatoes, all of which were expended at an extravagant party, for women, organized by the medium. Such outlays, I believe, are not unusual, even when the process of treatment is at its most informal. Since the treatment may not be successful, or may only temporarily alleviate the patient's afflictions – the possessing sprite being then said to be 'too strong' for the medium to control – repeated recourse to a succession of mediums inevitably involves considerable expenditure. In the case of married women, these unwelcomed responsibilities fall upon their husbands, and it is scarcely surprising, therefore, that these sprites are said generally to hate men. For these reasons, according to women, men must be excluded completely from the ceremonies.

The invoking of religion in the treatment of illness, and the use of modern Western medicine are not generally considered by Somali to be in any way incompatible and are regularly combined in treating disease. But in the case of *saar* affliction, treatment is wholly assigned to ceremonial exorcism, and is opposed to treatment by the world of men and to modern Western medicine.

Men in general are highly sceptical of women's sprite afflictions which they regard at best as malingering, and at worst as a pernicious extortion racket through which men are led to indulge their wives' insatiable demands for new clothes and delicate foods. Men support this view of the matter by pointing out how much more frequently the wives of the rich are smitten than those in poorer circumstances, a conclusion which is countered, as we have seen, by women's claims that there are two sorts of sprite – one for the rich and another for the poor.

In general, men show little patience when their own wives are subject to this costly affliction. Scepticism centres not only on the fact that it is generally rich women who are most often possessed, but also on the fact that the affliction is almost solely restricted to women (the *saar* possession of the camel-herder is, as we have seen, not considered seriously as an illness – nor does it involve financial outlays). For women are considered by men weak and foolish and easily swayed. The more general interpretation advanced here, namely, that the phenomenon must be seen as an aspect of the secluded social life of women, the constriction of the married woman's position, and her lack of other means for venting grievances, is also consistent with this emphasis on the 'weakness' of women. For it is their weakness in relation to the dominant males which makes them especially susceptible to mystical dangers. A quarrelsome and flighty wife is more liable to speedy divorce than one who takes refuge in spirit-possession, although, as has been seen, even this device must be used with moderation if it is not to provoke the same result.

It can be said that prevailing gender attitudes towards spirit affliction highlight the contrasting interests of women in *saar* and of men in the official cult of Islam. It is not inconsistent with this distinction that in the rare cases when illness in adult men is ascribed to spirit possession, the sprites involved should be those that are regarded as the learned sheikhs amongst jinns, which I refer to as 'learned' sprites (*wadaaddo*).[10]

POSSESSION BY 'LEARNED' SPRITES

These sprites, it is believed, strike men rather than women, causing possession with the same range of symptoms noted earlier, and in keeping with this gender distinction it is appropriate that they should be considered more deadly and dangerous than *saar* sprites since the threshold of resistance to mystical malignancy in such weak creatures as women is considered to be low. Here, as with *saar*, possession by these powerful demons is not attributed directly to any context of personal hostility between individuals or groups, although there is thought to be some danger of contagion which may be increased by hostility and bad feeling on the part of those already afflicted. Thus, not only can a man catch the disease from someone who is already suffering from it, but such transmission is likely to be encouraged if the two men quarrel or fight. Several people afflicted with this malady whom I encountered told me that they had 'caught' it from others suffering from it with whom they had fought, and it is believed to be particularly dangerous both to the possessed and to his assailant to strike an afflicted person on the shoulders.

It is clear, however, from the way in which this affliction is discussed and from the instances which I saw or heard of, that the precipitant leading to a diagnosis of possession by these sprites is always some particular hardship or deprivation or a deeply felt personal difficulty such as impotence. While I doubt if all the cases I know of involved real psychological disturbance or serious deficiencies in character (in terms of Somali values), such deviations, particularly where they are striking, are I think also likely to be referred to *wadaaddo* possession, and incline those so handicapped to resort to this affliction when they encounter insuperable difficulties. But in the absence of adequate information on the epidemiology of mental illness, it is difficult to pursue this theme further.

The element of deprivation which underlies all these cases is well represented in the following instance. A man I met told me that he was recurrently subject to possession by four 'learned' sprites (such multiple possession by *saar* in women is also encountered). They had originally attacked him when he was a boy of ten years old and was starving and hungry. Now, whenever he lacked food and help, they spoke to him, asking why he was starving them, why did he not give them tea and perfume? They also threatened him that if he did not give them perfume they would kill him. When this happens, if he has no money, he begs for help and buys perfume and food, then the sprites leave him. However, they also come back, he told me, when he is angry and begins quarreling and fighting. They say to him, 'Why are you fighting? We could kill you'. That these sprites should thus figure as being opposed to fighting is consistent with Somali conceptions of the pacific role of the holymen, of which they are the spiritual counterparts. And the implied connection between deprivation and fighting is very obvious to Somalis, however tenuous it may seem to others. For they see war, deprivation and drought as intimately related. It is lack of water and pasture for their herds which makes men hungry and bellicose, and regularly leads them in desperation to seek these necessities by force; and war itself, in turn, brings further desolation and misery. Thus war and drought are aptly contrasted in proverbs with peace and milk.

As with *saar* possession in women, this affliction is most effectively treated by those who have at one time suffered it, and who now hold 'authority' over it. This power, however, is limited appropriately enough to holymen who are the human equivalents of the sprites involved. The procedure usually followed is similar to that applied in the treatment of men who are possessed by a woman they have jilted. Thus the patient is swathed in blankets in a room with a fire on which incense is burnt, and verses from the Koran are recited against the possessing demon, which is exhorted to quit its victim. Again there is the dialogue between the spirit and the exorcist, and in this case especial difficulty may be encountered since this type of sprite is, as we have seen, credited with considerable knowledge of the Koran. In reality, of course, this can only be manifest when the patient himself is a sheikh, or one unusually well-educated in religion (which is not always the case). The inhalation of perfume is also (as with *saar*) considered helpful: and again, like *saar*, 'learned' sprites are sometimes said to favour red clothes, although I do not think that this is universally attributed to them or considered very important. Again, and in distinction to the treatment by holymen of diseases other than *wadaaddo*, recourse to a hospital is believed to be extremely dangerous. Thus, in a number of cases, patients suffering from pneumonia have been removed from hospital by their relatives, on the advice of a holyman claiming power over the sprites, sometimes with fatal results.

While *saar* possession is a well-established phenomenon in northern Somaliland, and although its precise antiquity is unknown, *wadaaddo* seems to be a more recent importation: generally, indeed, it is said to have entered the centre and west of the country from the east since the turn of the century. This process is described in such a way as to suggest that the affliction is pictured as an infection, gradually spreading westwards from the east, and its origin is universally traced to the Majerteen province where it is connected with Sultan 'Isman, the redoubtable clan-head of the Majerteen clan who was deposed by the Italians in 1927 when they seized control of this part of their former colony.

The stories which attest this attribution vary considerably in details, but all versions emphasize two themes. These are, first, that these sprites were formerly the spirit familiars of the Sultan – they are often described as his 'soldiers' – and on his deposition were released to trouble mankind generally; and second, that they are also in some way directly connected with a small Majerteen lineage of sheikhs and holymen, called the Fiqi Buuraaleh. This is a priestly group which has a very high reputation in mystical power, corresponding to its weakness in numbers and secular power. Cerulli, for example (1964, p.158), writing apparently of the situation in the late nineteen twenties, reports that this lineage is credited with the power of protecting crops from devastation by sparrows – a miraculous power attributed to such other, unrelated priestly lineages amongst the southern Somali cultivators as the Reer Sheikh Muumin (cf. above, Ch. 6). Thus, in the centre and west, far from any zone of actual contact with, or direct knowledge of this lineage, *wadaaddo* sprites are sometimes referred to as Reer Fiqi Buuraaleh, as though they represented a mystical line of holymen which maliciously, and capriciously visited men with sickness. And sometimes the human Reer Fiqi Buuraaleh are referred to as possessing the greatest power in controlling and curing the disease ascribed to them.

It is important to emphasize that this 'learned' sprites affliction is never ascribed to any other priestly group, or to the activities of holymen in general who, as we have seen, are generally credited with using the curse and sorcery to protect their persons and property from attack by warriors. It thus appears that the Reer Fiqi Buuraaleh, having acquired a wide reputation for their mystical efficacy, reinforced by their association with Sultan 'Isman, his conquests and fierce resistance to the Italians have, in an inter-clan context of hostility between the Majerteen and their neighbours, come to be regarded as a source of generalized malign influence. This interpretation, at least, is supported by the ascription of responsibility for the most deadly form of *saar* possession ('*saar Habashi*') to the Ethiopians in the context of Somali-Ethiopian hostility.

CONCLUSIONS

Although spirit possession in Somaliland is seen traditionally by many as a specific type of malady on a par with other known diseases, and ultimately most closely related to madness,[11] it is, as I have argued here, rather an explanation which is invoked to interpret real, or assumed, physical or psychological symptoms in a number of fairly clearly defined contexts. To understand these contexts it is necessary to appreciate that Muslim theology, as the Somali interpret it, presents the problem of a divinity who is responsible both for happiness and affliction and whose rewards and punishments fall due in the after-life rather than in this. The gulf in the moral evaluation of human interaction which this creates, is partly filled by the readiness with which antagonisms and tensions are ventilated by direct recourse to physical combat. But, not everyone can be secularly powerful and secure; envy and covetousness consequently cannot be excluded, and there remains a general notion of mystical influence as the ultimate resource of the downtrodden and weak. This assumes a variety of forms – the curse, sorcery, the evil eye, and spirit possession – each associated with different cultural contexts and structural situations. The last, however, is only mobilized in a limited number of culturally defined circumstances which involve the underlying element of powerlessness and which, for the most part, are concerned with relations between the sexes.

It is in this sense, rather than in any holistic one that these beliefs, which ethnographically are part of the Somali religion, are, as it were, tailored to the social structure and system of values. The characteristics attributed to the spirit entities involved, cannot themselves be seen as exactly mirroring the social structure in which they serve as objectifications of fear and envy, for spirit possession is very far from being at the centre of the official cult. And in any case, many of their attributes derive directly from the religious heritage of Islam, although they are not identical in all respects with those found in the beliefs of other Muslim peoples (see, e.g., Westermarck, 1926). It might even seem that the problem which relative deprivation poses is inherent in the Somali scheme of values and presents what might be described as a loophole through which new beliefs (such, for example, as *wadaaddo*) may readily be absorbed to explain, and in some cases actually to remedy, afflictions of this kind. Unfortunately, of course, we do not know what happened before *wadaaddo* or *saar* made their appearance, and there is little point in speculating.

In the absence of adequate psychological evidence also, it is likewise difficult to assess the extent to which those who seek these remedies in the culturally appropriate situation, are in fact subject to real mental disturbance or illness. But it appears, at least in my experience, that those who are especially susceptible to possession are constitutionally, or feel they are, least able to cope adequately with the pressures and ideal standards of the pastoral life which is their lot. Thus, not only women in general who in relation to men are considered to be intrinsically weak, but women with particular burdens or personality problems, seem those most prone recurrently to seek this solution to the difficulties they experience in such a male-dominated society. This is particularly clear in the case of those women who regularly succumb to possession, and find security as professional mediums. I think also that those men who are regularly affected by the affliction attributed to clerical sprites probably have similar difficulties. It is consequently tempting to compare the epidemiology of *saar* possession in Somali women with the incidence of depression and other mental illnesses of women in depressed circumstances elsewhere. Certainly there is much to suggest that the Somali woman often finds herself trapped in circumstances from which there seems to be no easy line of escape except through what men unsympathetically assume to be a form of malingering. This, at any rate, is thoroughly consistent with the character of the relations between the sexes in traditional Somali society. And it is therefore scarcely surprising that spirit possession should also be linked with the covert and indirect expression of emotion – whether of love or hate – between men and women.

Today this old pastoral order is changing. In towns particularly, the relations between men and women are freer than formerly and such topics as the general enfranchisement of women, freedom to contract love matches, and the direct expression of love and its acknowledgement as an honourable sentiment are all hotly debated, not least in the press and on the radio.[12] At the same time, the modern 'pop' song (*heelo*) which has evolved in the 1940s and 1950s to become widely listened to on the radio in both town and interior, treats freely and directly of love and passion in a manner which many of the guardians of the old order find shameful and disgusting (c.f. the poem 'The evils of the Balwo', Andrezejewski and Lewis, 1964, 151-152; see also, Johnson, 1996). It is highly significant for our analysis, moreover, that in these modern songs, men and women are described as smitten and held in thrall by love in precisely that terminology which is traditionally employed in the corresponding contexts of spirit possession. Despite these developments, belief in *saar* sprites, although waning, has not disappeared, and they continue to be invoked in cases of personal difficulty (as e.g. in post-1990 refugee camps). The accompanying dance is also, I think, increasingly acquiring popularity as a form of spectacle, or entertainment in towns.

Notes

1   Doctor R. E. Drake-Brockmann, a medical officer with long experience in northern Somaliland, describes these and other procedures, including the insertion of animal bones in shattered bone structures, in his book (1912, 156-162).

2   For some indication of the range of traditional diagnostic knowledge and the wealth of terms in Somali for locally ocurring diseases and medical processes, see M. Maino (1953).

3   Thus, as early as 1854, Richard Burton noted skeptically that Somalis associated malaria with the bite of the mosquito, and attributed this 'superstition' to the fact that 'mosquitos and fevers become formidable about the same time' (Burton, 1943, 33).

4   *Wadaaddo* is the plural of *wadaad*, the Somali equivalent of the Arabic sheikh or *fiqi*, meaning a holyman, one learned in religion. The singular form is *not* used of these 'learned' sprites.

5   For a fuller analysis of northern Somali social structure, see Lewis 1961.

6   Other related meanings of the verb *qab* are to marry (man speaking), and more generally to have, hold, or do.

7   The theme of a popular play by Abdi Rodol, broadcast on the Somali service of the BBC concerns the unhappy plight of a love-sick girl whose father refuses to allow her to marry the man of her choice. She falls sick and is treated for spirit-possession, but this brings no relief. At last her true condition is correctly diagnosed by a learned sheikh who persuades her father to agree to the marriage she desires.

8   This refers to the practice common among young men of bleaching their hair. 'White-haired boys' is, however, also a synonym for the *saar* dance.

9   In 1953 one such youth attending a boy's boarding school in northern Somaliland, when stimulated to a pitch of frenzy by *saar* songs sung to him by his high-school fellows, seized an axe and killed one of his companions. The boy was tried for homicide in a court and a plea of temporary insanity was accepted on the evidence of a medical witness who testified that the accused was suffering from a form of epilepsy. The boy explained that he was safe as long as he was wearing a protective amulet containing verses from the Koran. He had not been wearing this at the time of the murder. (cf. Ross, 1956).

10   These are also sometimes called *'ardoyin', from 'ardo'*, a student of religion. This particular plural, however, unlike the word *wadaaddo*, is only applied to these sprites and never to their human counterparts.

11   Madness may also be caused, it is believed, by excessive absorption in religious devotion. Thus there are many clerics, often disparagingly called 'Sufis' (i.e. Mystics) by Somalis, who exhibit similar hysterical symptoms at religious ceremonies to those of the *saar*-possessed camel herders. These are seldom treated with much respect, but regarded rather as crazy fanatics suffering from what secular Westerners might call religious mania.

12   For an interesting, revealing, and remarkably frank correspondence on

the subject of 'love', see *The Somali News*, 1964, all weekly issues for July-September, especially that of August 21.

Appendix 1

THE NAMES OF GOD IN NORTHERN SOMALI[1]

Amongst the Somali, God is universally known by the names Allah[2] and Rabbi, both of Arabic origin, but the full list of His 99 Arabic names is known only to sheikhs and *wadaads*.[3] In addition to the Arabic names, however, there are a considerable number of purely Somali titles for Allah. The majority of those recorded here will be seen to be praise-names referring to God's attributes and in many cases direct equivalents in Somali of the corresponding titles in Arabic. The following list compiled initially by Yuusuf Maygaag,[4] for some time my research associate, and a recognized authority on Somali culture and language, does not pretend to be exhaustive.

1. *Baahilaawe* 'He who is without need or want', Who is self-sufficient; from *baahi-da* 'need' or 'want', and *laawe* 'without'. Cf. Ar. *Al-Ghaniyy*.[5] There is a well-known Somali spirit-possession dance known as *baahilaawe* or *baloolay* (also *baar*

---

1 There are slight dialectal differences in the Somali spoken by the 'Iise (Esa), Gadabuursi (both Dir), the Isaaq, Daarood, and northern Hawiye, but these differences are slight in comparison with those between 'Northern Somali', spoken by these groups as a whole, and 'Southern Somali', spoken by the Rahanwiin and Digil, the people of the Banaadir Coast, and the southern Hawiye. Cf. M. M. Moreno, *Il Somalo della Somalia*, Roma, 1955, 3-22; B.W. Andrzejewski and M. H. I. Galaal, *Hikmad Soomaali*, O.U.P., 1956, p. 1.
2 *Illaah*, and *Illaahi*, also occur in Somali.
3 The word *wadaad-ka* is used synonimously with *sheikh*, although strictly the latter is applied to a man whose knowledge of the Shariah is more advanced than that of a wadaad.
4 Of the Sa'ad Muuse, Abdalla Sa'ad lineage of the Habar Awal clan (Isaaq) of the British Protectorate.
5 In giving the Somali titles for God I do not include the definite article because contrary to the Arabic convention this is not good Somali usage.

'adde),[6] which seems to have arisen from a particular cult or *dhikri*, but hardly a new *tariiqa*, founded perhaps some 200 years ago by a man of the Ogaadeen Reer 'Abdille[7] lineage. But *Baahilaawe* as a name of God may well have existed long before its use in this particular form of praise.

3. *Bogsiiye* 'the Curer, the Healer'; from *bogsii* (v.) 'cure, make better, deliver from misfortune'. Cf. Ar. *Al-Shafi*.

4. *Dile* 'the Killer, He who causes death'; from *dil* (v.) 'kill, cause death of' – used of man as agent as well as God. Cf. Ar. *Al-Mumit*.

5. *Eebbe* 'Master, Lord'. With *Waaq* (see below) the direct Somali correspondence to the Ar. Allah.

6. *Guulle* 'the Victor, He who gives victory'; from *guul-sha* 'victory'. Cf. Ar. *Al-Nasir*.

7. *Hagaaje* or *Hagaajiye* 'the Amender, the Corrector, He who leads to the right path'; from *hagaag-ga* 'the right, the straightened', *hagaagi* (v.) 'straighten, amend, put right'. Cf. Ar. *Al-Hadi*.

8. *Hanuunshe* 'He who leads to the Right Way'; from *hanuun-ka* 'the correct path, the right way', opposite of astray. Cf. Ar. *Al-Hadi*.

9. *Hidije* or (in north-west) *Kare* 'the Bestower of Bounties, He 'who has power to bestow'; from *hidis-ka* or *hidin-ta* 'the ability to do or bestow'; and *karti-da* 'power to do'. Cf. Ar. *Al-Qadir*.

10. *Hodmiye* or *Badaadshe* 'the Enricher, Creator of Wealth'; from *hodmi* (v.) 'enrich, satisfy', and *badaadi* (v.) 'enrich, satisfy'. Cf. Ar. *Al-Mughni*.

---

6 Baalolay-da, a she-camel which is not pregnant. The dance is said to have acquired this name by its initiator Sheikh Bahilaawe through his having on a certain occasion slaughtered a *baloolay* camel for a party of sheikhs who visited him. It was after this great gesture of hospitality to the *'ulimo* that God gave him wisdom and knowledge of the Shariah and inspired him to create the *dhikri* by which he is known as Sheikh Baloolay or Bahilaawe.

7 The Reer Abdille are a large lineage of the Ogaadeen clan of the Daarood clan-family living in the Ogaden region to the south of the British Protectorate. On the Daarood see I. M. Lewis, *Peoples of the Horn of Africa: Somali, Afar and Saho*, 1994, 18-23.

11. *Kaalmeeye* or *Gargaare* 'the Helper'; from *kaalmo-ha, gargaar-ka,* 'help' or 'assistance'. Cf. Ar. *Al-Mu'in.*

12. *Koobe* 'the Accounter, the Numberer'; *koob* (v.) 'count, enumerate, know number of'. Cf. Ar. *Al-Muhsi.*

13. *Korreeye* or *Sarreeye* 'He who is On High'; from *kor-ka* 'top', *sare* 'on top of'. Cf. Ar. *Al- 'aliyy.*

14. *Madinte* 'the Everlasting, He who Does Not Die'; from *dimo* (v.) 'die', *ma* 'not'. Cf. Ar. *Al-Hayy.*

15. *Mahadaale* or *Galladaale* 'He to whom Thanks must be Given'; from *mahad-da* or *gallad-da* 'thanks'. Cf. *Ar. Al-Shakur.*

16. *Nooleeye* 'the Creator, the Giver of Life, the Reviver'; from *nolol-sha* 'life'. Cf. Ar. *Al-Muhi.*

17. *Roone* 'the Generous, the Most Beneficent'; from *roone* (adj.) 'generous, beneficent, strong (in the sense of numerous)', as e.g. *wuu ka roonyahay* 'he is better, greater, stronger, etc.', *hoogroone,* 'stronger' (as e.g. of two parties). Cf. Ar. *Al-Karim.*

18. *Sameeye* or *Abuure* 'Maker, Creator'; from *samee* (v.) 'do, make (from something)', *abuur* (v.) 'create *(ex nihilo)*'. *Samee* has the sense of to fashion from already existing material, while *abuur* is to create from nothing and is only applied to God. Thus for example 'I begot (children) but God created (or gave me) them' is in Somali, *anigaa dalay Ilaahay baase abuuray.* In this sense the verb *abuur* describes God's precedence in all creative acts or growth; all ultimately spring only from Him. Cf. Ar. *Al-Khaliq.*

19. *Siiye* 'Giver', He who grants; *sii* (v.) 'give'. Cf. Ar. *Al-Wahhab* and *Al-Mu'ti.*

20. *Ururiye* or *Ururshe* 'the Gatherer', He who summons the dead to account; from *urur* (v.) 'collect' or 'gather', inanimate or animate objects. Cf. Ar. *Al-Jami '.*

21. *Waaq* or *Waaqa* 'God' cf. *Eebbe* corresponding exactly to Ar. Allah. This word is further discussed below.

22. *Waare* or *Jire* 'the Eternal', 'He who lives for ever'; from *waar* (v.) 'to be eternal', applied only to God, and *jir* (v.) 'be', or 'live', applied equally to persons and things and only in a special sense to God. Cf. Ar. *Al-Baqi.*

23. *Weyne* 'the Great, Immense'; from *weyn* 'big' or 'large', etc. Cf. Ar. *Al-Kabir* and *Al-Azim.*

With the exception of *Eebbe* generally these names are rarely used although they sometimes occur in proper and place names, in swearing, in poetry and song and in certain religious expressions. They are, however, particularly used by sheikhs and *wadaads* in interpreting in Somali the various qualities of Allah. In their etymology they represent the Somali interpretation of Muslim theosophy. It seems impossible to know definitely whether or not they were all applied to God in pre-Islamic times, likely though this appears in some if not all cases. But they are certainly generally regarded as being very old.

The name *Waaq* (Cf. Oromo *Waaqa*)[8] is especially interesting. Cerulli[9] has indicated something of the probable nature of the pre-Islamic cult of the Cushitic God *Waaq*[10] and I have attempted[11] to discuss Somali Sufism in terms of syncretism to it. Today northern Somaliland is solidly and deeply Muslim and while, as in all countries, there still survive various practices and superstitions regarded by Somali as pre-Islamic,[12] *Waaq* is no longer venerated. I have never heard Allah addressed directly as *Waaq* although he is sometimes addressed as *Eebbe*. The name *Waaq* survives, however, and is regarded by Somali as an ancient pre-Islamic name for God. Its use by the non-Muslim Oromo is well known to Somali but is not considered by them to have been introduced from Oromo. As well as being an old name for God in northern Somali, the name occurs also in several compound words. Cerulli[13] has instanced its occurrence in proper names such as: *Waaqsuge* (or *Waassuge* equivalent to

---

8 See G.B.W. Huntingford, *The Galla of Ethiopia.- The Kingdoms of Kafa and Janjero*, London, 1955, 74-87.

9 E. Cerulli, *RSO*, x, 1923, 1-36.

10 I do not wish to imply that *Waaq* is the only name for the Cushitic God, or indeed the only Cushitic God, but that this word is one of the Cushitic names for God in Oromo and Somali.

11 Chapter 1, above.

12 I refer here only to ritual, magical, and religious phenomena. The interaction of the Shari'a and secular Somali custom is a vast and complex subject. Various practices regarded as superstitious, and by some as unorthodox, have also been introduced with Islam from Arabia. Fortune-telling by the beads of the rosary and other means, in Somali *faal-ka*, is of Arabian origin (Cf. Ar. *fa'l*). Contrast Somali sorcery, *fal-ka*, corresponding to the Ar. *sihr*. Arabic words of astrology, medicine and magic such as *Kitab al-Rahma*, by Jelal al-Din 'Abd al-Rahman al-Suyuti, Cairo, 1938, are very popular in Somaliland and much of the terminology of such practices is Arabic.

13 Cerulli, op. cit., 5.

Allaahsuge) 'he who waits for God', *Dardaar Waaq* 'adherent of God',[14] *Ga'alWaaq* 'God's love'.[15] Other clan-names which include *Waaq* are: *JidWaaq* 'the path of God',[16] *TagaalWaaq* 'follower of God',[17] *'Aabud-Waaq* 'he who worships God'.[18]

Other more interesting uses are in phrases like *weligaa iyo Waaqaa* (exactly equivalent to *weligaa iyo Allaahaa*) meaning 'never before, never in your life', as in the sentence, *weligay iyo Waaqay kaas oo maan arag* 'I have never seen anything like that in all my life', or *Waaqay maan arag* 'I have never seen before'. One may also say, *Waaq annu soo noqonnin* (exactly equivalent to *Illaahow aanu soo noqonnin*) 'May he never return', 'Let God not bring him back'. The name *Waaq* also occurs in the following mat-weaving song, sung both in the east and west of northern Somaliland by women as they make *'aws* or *harrar*[19] *mats. This is a 'Hoyal'* song (*hees*-ta) named after the character of the refrain in which '*hoyal*' is repeated and it is worth quoting here in its entirety.

'*Awskanow sabool*[20] *diidow,*
Waaq an suuka lagu digin oon,

---

14 In Northern Somali *dardaaran-ka* is the last will or testamentary disposition of property made orally by a man in the presence of kinsmen and *wadaads* who are charged to see that his terms are fulfilled. *Dardaar* is applied (as an adjective) as a name for the last child of a family of children begotten of the same parents; it has the sense of 'the last of God's blessing'.
15 From *ga'al-ka* 'love'.
16 From *jid-ka* 'road, path, way'. The *JidWaaq* are a Daarood clan living mainly as cultivators to the East of Harar in Ethiopia, whither they were driven from their original home in north-eastern Somaliland probably in the sixteenth century; see Lewis, op. cit., 21.
17 From the verb *tag* 'go'. The TagalWaaq are a Daarood clan living today in the western Ogaden between Jigjiga and Harar. Some are found also with the Habar Awal (Isaaq) with whom they pay blood-money (mag-ta), in the British Protectorate.
18 From *'aabud-ka* 'fearer, worshipper', cf. Ar. 'abid. The *'AabudWaaq* are a Daarood clan, today inhabiting northern Kenya to the north-east of the Tana River. For the movement of the Daarood into this region see Lewis, op.cit., 47-8.
19 *'Aws-ka* is grass in general, including many separate named varieties and also with harrar-ka the general name for those mats woven principally from grass and used in the construction of the walls and roof of the Somali house. These naturally differ in design and quality.
20 *Sabool-ka* 'poor, destitute', perhaps connected with *sabo-da*, a patch of parched-grass exhausted by over-grazing near a well where stock water.

Soddon lagugu baayi'in[21] oon,
Yaa sameeyay lagu udanney,
Ey hooyalaayow, hoyal
Ey hooyalow hooyee,
Hoyalley.[22]
This mat is not for a poor man,
God forbid that I should have to take it to the market,
Thirty (Rupees) could not buy it,
'Who made it?' they will ask.
Ey hooyalaayow... (equivalent to 'La, la, la...').

The Somali expression for abundance and plenty, the time after the rains and abundant water and grass when none go without, is *barwaaqo-da,* as opposed to drought and famine (*abaar-ta*). This word is regarded as being very old and appears to be a compound of *bar-ta* 'a spot of rain' or 'property' and *Waaqa* 'God'. This is certainly the only satisfactory etymology which I have been offered by Somali.[23] Although they tell us little of its nature, such usages provide evidence of a former cult of the Cushitic God *Waaq* in northern Somaliland. But in this region it is not under this name that God is now worshipped.

In central and southern Somalia in the area occupied by the Hawiye[24] clan-family, the impression is gained that Islam although strongly developed, is not perhaps quite as deeply rooted as

---

21 Verb from *baaya 'ad-da* 'bargaining' or 'selling'. Cf. Ar. *bay'.*

22 '*Hoyal'* is the leading word of the refrain sung at the end of each line by the companions of the soloist. The last three lines are the chorus. The song is transcribed here as it would be sung, and was originally recorded amongst the Dulbahante (Daarood) in the east of the British Protectorate. But it is well known generally in the Protectorate.

23 Large spots of rain are *barweyn,* small spots *baryar.* Bar (pl. *baro-ha*) means also any small spot in general, as e.g. a mark on the skin. Bar-ta (pl. *bar-ta*) 'property' in general, including immovable and movable property and livestock; cf, *barlaawe* 'without property, property-less'. *Barwaaq* 'prosperous, lucky, blessed', as in *BarWaaq,* a nickname of the founding ancestor of the Ogaadeen clan.

24 For the Hawiye see Lewis, op. cit., 28-31.

in northern Somaliland.[25] This is also, of course, particularly true of the Bantu riverine people of the Shabelle and Juba region, but as they are of non-Somali (and non-Cushitic) origin, survivals of pre-Islamic beliefs amongst them are not relevant to a discussion of pre-Islamic Somali survivals. Nor is consideration of the Digil and Rahanwiin (Sab)[26] clan-families of southern Somalia apposite here, for in their present extremely mixed clan constitution they are of relatively recent formation and contain many Oromo (Borana and other Oromo) elements.[27] It is probable, therefore, that any traces amongst the Sab of the cult of *Waaq* would be of recent Oromo introduction and throw little or no direct light upon pre-Muslim Somali religion.

Features of Hawiye belief and religious practice, especially of the Agbaal clan (living along the coast and to a considerable extent inland, to the north of Mogadishu), which appear to be connected with a pre-Islamic cult of *Waaq* have been noticed by Cerulli.[28] The most significant is the use of the expression *Waaqda'in*,[29] one of many Hawiye expressions for sacrifice, or offering, to God. Other

---

25 Islam was, according to the testimony of Arab historians, established on the Somali coast by the ninth to tenth century, see chapter 1, above. To what if any considerabe extent it had at this date penetrated into the interior is difficult to assess. All the Somali clans and clan-families claim ultimately to be of Arabian origin although the extent to which they stress such claims varies considerably. [The cult of the Hawiye eponym as a Sufi saint is certainly less developed than that of Sheikh Daarood, who probably reached Somaliland from Arabia around the eleventh century, or of Sheikh Isaaq (founder of the Isaaq clan-family) whose date of arrival from Arabia is ascribed to the thirteenth century. According to Shariif 'Aydaruus Shariif 'Ali's *Bughyat al-amaal fii taariqh as-Somaal*, Mogadishu, 1955, 279-81, the eponym 'Samaale' himself emigrated from the Yemen to Somaliland in the ninth century. At any rate, as the Daarood and Isaaq were driven southwords in the direction of their present habitat, and, if the traditions of their Arabian origin are correct, must have originally been Muslim. Their contact with Arabia and Islam may thereafter have decreased in their subsequent migrations. To-day in dress, hair-styles, and other habits, they still adhere as a whole more closely to traditional Somali custom than do either the Daarood or Isaaq.]

26 For a summary history of the Sab, see Lewis, op. cit., 46-8, etc.

27 See M. Colucci, *Principi di diritto consuetudinario della Somalia italiana meridionale*, Firenze, 1924, 119-39.

28 Cerulli, op. cit., 6-9.

29 From *Waaq* and *du'ayn* (v.) 'to bless, pray for'; the noun is *du'o-dda*. Cf. Ar. *du 'a'*. Cerulli, op. cit., gives the form *Waaqda'il*, and not *Waaqda'in*, as I have heard it. M. M. Moreno, op. cit., 224, records *Waaqda'in* from an Ashraaf informant of the Reer Hamar clan of Mogadishu.

equivalent words in Hawiye are *durraamo*,[30] *Rabbituug*,[31] *Rabbibari*, *and Allaahbari*. The two last mean literally 'to beseech God' (from *bari* (v.) 'beseech, beg') and are applied universally in Somaliland to any type of sacrifice or offering to God. In Northern Somaliland, the Hawiye *Waaqda'in* is unknown, and indeed unintelligible, to the majority. Further research amongst the Hawiye (or the Dir),[32] especially amongst those Hawiye living relatively sheltered from external influence along the Ethiopian border of Somalia or in northern Kenya, may reveal more definite traces of the cult of *Waaq surviving from pre-Islamic times.*

---

30 *Durraamo* (v.) 'beseech, beg repeatedly, implore', as *Waan ku durraamaneyaa* 'I implore you'. The noun is *durraamusho-da* 'beseeching, prayer'. Cf. the proverbial phrase, *Shaydaan naftiisaa janno loo duurraantaa* 'The devil is implored to enter Heaven' (but he always refuses).

31 From *Rabbi* 'God' and *tuug* (v.) 'ask for, pray'. The difference between this word and *tuug-ga* 'thief' is that the vowel sound in the second is pronounced with 'fronting'. According to Andrzejewski, *BSOAS*, XVII, 3, 1955, 567-80.

32 The strongest and largest present-day representatives of the Dir clan-family are the 'Iise and Gadabuursi of northern Somaliland, who have, for the most part, lost their traditions of Dir origin. The Isaaq, who are considered by other Somali to be of Dir origin, claim themselves to be *Ashraaf*, see Lewis, *The Somali Lineage System and the Total Genealogy* (duplicated), Hargeisa, 1957, where these rival claims are discussed in their social contexts. Other small groups of Dir origin survive all over Somaliland and especially in southern Somalia. The Dir are generally regarded as the oldest Somali Group.

The 'Iise and Gadabuursi, devout Muslims though they are, are perhaps the least deeply Islamized of the northern Somali and certainly many pre-Islamic Somali customs survive amongst them in greater clarity than they do among the Isaaq or Daarood. But while working amongst them I could find no traces of any cult of *Waaq*. More thorough and extended research into their religious practice might yield traces of religious beliefs connected with *Waaq*.

Appendix II

New Arabic Documents from Somalia

B.W. Andrzejewski and I.M.Lewis

ORIGIN OF THE COLLECTION

While carrying out social anthropological research among the northern, largely pastoralist Somali in what was then the Somaliland Protectorate between 1955 and 1957, one of us, (see Lewis, 1961; 1982) attempted to discover and collect as much written, mainly religious, material as possible. The aim was to illuminate and to document the literate Islamic tradition which in an important sense underpins this essentially oral culture (cf. Lewis 1968 and 1986).

As Lewis soon discovered, much of the Arabic manuscript material he could locate in the private libraries of sheikhs, could not be directly acquired or photocopied. Nor, indeed, would it have been ethically appropriate to seek to persuade their possessors to part with such treasured items even for a few hours. Accordingly, Lewis adopted the device of employing Somali research assistants literate in Arabic to copy such material as he could discover in the course of his researches in north-western Somalia.

RELEVANCE OF THE DOCUMENTS AS RESEARCH MATERIALS

Although the material is not in any sense comprehensive, or statistically representative, we believe it contains important new evidence for understanding Somali Islam and contributes to a fuller documentation of this vital aspect of Somali culture and history. The tragic conflicts and chaos of the late 1980s in northern Somalia (now the self-declared 'Somaliland Republic') make this material all the more precious. Particularly in these circumstances, it seems high time to make these documents available to other scholars by depositing copies in several appropriate libraries. As a prelude to this, it has seemed logical for us to prepare the catalogue, which is given in this paper, for the benefit of our colleagues. The originals are now in the Manuscript Section of the Library of the London School of Economics and Political Science, University of London.

CONTENT CHARACTERISTICS OF THE DOCUMENTS

As will be apparent, the bulk of our texts reflects the strong emphasis on Sufism in Somali Islam (cf. Lewis 1955b and 1956, Martin 1976 and 1992) and consists of hagiographical *qasidas* in praise of the founders of *tariiqas* followed by Somalis (mainly the Qaadiriya and Saalihiya), of local Somali saints connected with *tariiqas*, and of the clan ancestors whom Somalis venerate as saints. As illuminating particular aspects of Somali culture, we would draw attention specially to the prayers composed and sung by women (MS 5), the critical discussion and letter concerning the Somali Dervish leader Sayyid Mahammad 'Abd Allaah Hasan (MS 18), his biography (MS 22(a)), the accounts of Somali *tariiqas* (MS 21) and the important, perhaps unique, historical material on the Saalihiya *tariiqa* and its founder, (MS 22(b)), the records of the Dervish War (MS 25), the very rare documentation in MS 26 on the cult of the lineage ancestor of the Midgan occupational caste (cf. Lewis 1955a pp.51-56, 1961 p.188), and finally two printed pamphlets, the first extolling the religious power of Sheikh Ismaail Jabarti, the putative ancestor of the Daarood clan family, and the second praising Sheikh Isaaq, founder of the clan-family named after him.

PLACE OF THE DOCUMENTS WITHIN SOMALI LITERARY CULTURE

The documents in the present collection, with the exception of MS 5 and Item (j) in MS 26, and of those items marked with the abbreviation "Extr. m." (Extraneous matter), belong to the Somali literature in Arabic. While most of it consists of manuscripts, a small proportion has appeared in printed books and pamphlets, and information concerning this literature is provided in Cerulli (1957), Andrzejewski (1974 and 1983), Mohamed Haji Mukhtar (1987), Alawi Ali Adan (1992), Martin 1976 and 1992) and Said S. Samatar (1992).

MS 5 and Item (j) in MS 26 represent literature written in Somali but using Arabic characters. This branch of Somali literature is much less extensive but has received attention in Cerulli (1964), Moreno (1955), Abdisalam Yassin Mohamed (1977) and Banti (1987).

Items marked as "Extr. m." found themselves in the collection by accident, the copyists or their friends having used the paper of the manuscripts for drafting letters or making personal notes. This is not surprising if we take into account the cost of paper when the documents were copied.

While most of the manuscripts are clearly written and conform well to the norms of Arabic grammar, syntax and calligraphy, some deviate so substantially as to be extremely difficult to decipher. In this connection we acknowledge our indebtedness to Mahammad Dahir Afrah and Mohamoud Sheikh Dalmar for their most valuable help. We also gratefully acknowledge the financial assistance given to us during the preparation of this material by the Staff Research Fund of the London School of Economics and Political Science.

METHODS USED IN CATALOGUING THE COLLECTION

The catalogue is not arranged according to any thematic or genre classification, since it would have been difficult to do so on account of great variety of items in some manuscripts. The term *qasida*, abbreviated to the single capital letter Q, is restricted here to religious poems, in accordance with the usage prevalent among Somalis, and the term poem is applied to compositions which fall outside that definition. The title Sheikh, which is abbreviated here to Sh., refers to learned men of religion and not to any secular leaders. By the expression "Q to" is meant that the main theme of praise and supplication is addressed to a particular holy person or to God. Thus, for example, "Q to Sh.Isaaq" should be interpreted as "*Qasida* of praise and supplication addressed to Sh. Isaaq". It should be noted that in addition the opening and closing lines of all poems normally contain praises and supplications addressed to God. They also contain salutations to Mahammad, by which religious poets greet their beloved Prophet.

When no authorship is given for a particular item this merely means that it is not stated in the manuscript and does not necessarily imply that it circulated among Somalis as an anonymous work. When two persons are named as authors it is not certain which is the author and which the copyist.

Most manuscripts have no titles and it is very difficult to identify them individually without a considerable amount of elaboration which is beyond the scope of this catalogue. *Qasidas* in this collection, even if they are addressed to the same person, all have different individual texts. Some set common phrases and images, however, are frequently shared in them.

The sizes of the documents are given in centimetres.

THE CATALOGUE

Manuscripts

MS 1
6pp. 16.3 x 20.5

A group of short *qasidas* which are sung at religious meetings, in part with the accompaniment of drumming.

(a) Q to Sh. 'Abd al-Qaadir al-Jilaani.
(b) Q as in (a).
(c) Q as in (a).
(d) Q the wording of which does not make clear to whom it is addressed (probably: as in (a)).
(e) Q to Mahammad.

The *qasidas* in this group use intoxication with wine as their imagery for ecstatic states.

MS 2
22 pp. 16.3 x 20.5

(a) 'Abd al-Raaziq al-Tajurri al-Dankali: Q to Sh. Isaaq bin Ahmad.
(b) Sh. Ahmad Bilah Daraar and Sh. Ahmad Ruublah: Q as in (a).
(c) Sh. 'Abd Allaah Warsamah and 'Abd al-Raaziq al-Dankali: Q to Sh. 'Abd al-Rahmaan bin Ahmad al-Zayla'i.
(d) Sh. 'Abd Allaah Warsamah and 'Abd al-Raaziq al-Dankali: Q as in (a).
(e) Sh. 'Abd Allaah Warsamah and 'Abd al-Raaziq al-Dankali: Q as in (c).
(f) Sh. Ahmad bin Ruublah: Q as in (a) and in praise of his progeny.
(g) Sh. Ahmad bin Ruublah: Q as in (a).
(h) Sh. Ahmad bin Ruublah: Q as in (a).
(i) Sh. Ahmad bin Ruublah: Q as in (a).

MS 3
19 pp. 16.3 x 20.5

(a) Sh. Mahammad ibn 'Ali (probably only the copyist): Q to Mahammad (fragment).

(b) Sh. 'Abd al-Rahmaan al-Zayla'i: Q to Mahammad.
(c) Sh. Yuusuf al-Bahr: Q to Sh. 'Abd al-Qaadir al-Jilaani.
(d) Q to Sh. 'Abd al-Qaadir al-Jilaani.
(e) Sh. Mahmuud Warsamah: Q as in (b).
(f) Sh. 'Abdi Hiruus (or Hiraws): Q to Sh.Yuusuf al-Kawnayn
     (also known as Sh. Yuusuf al-Akwaan and Aw Barkhadlah).
(g) Sh. Mahmuud Warsamah: Q as in (b).
(h) Names of sheikhs venerated as saints and the locations of
     their activities.

MS 4
13 pp. 16.3 x 20.5

(a) Q to Sh. 'Abd al-Qaadir al-Jilaani.
(b) List of sheikhs venerated as saints, identical with that in MS
     3, item (h).
(c) Q to Sh. Isaaq ibn Ahmad.
(d) Q as in (c).
(e) Q as in (c).
(f) Q to Sh. Nuur 'Uthmaan.

MS 5
4 pp. 15.8 x 20.4

The texts in this MS are in Somali written in Arabic characters.
They consist of four prayers sung by women in the Somali poetic
genre called *buraanbur*. The transcription is very inadequate since it
ignores the essential sound distinctions of Somali phonology. It is
not certain whether the women who dictated the texts were authors
or merely reciters.

(a) Indhadeeq, (transcriber 'Ali Muusa): Prayer to Faatimah.
(b) Prayer to Mahammad.
(c) Bugir (or Bugyar): A prayerful meditation.
(d) Kaaha Shaykh: Prayer to Hawaa (Eve).

MS 6
30 pp. 18 x 26

(a) Short pious invocation to Mahammad.
(b) Extr. m.: Draft of a private letter the subject of which is diffi-
     cult to ascertain since its context is unknown.
(c) Q to Sh. Isaaq bin Ahmad.
(d) Q as in (c).
(e) Q welcoming the arrival of the month of Ramadan.

(f)   Q to Sh. 'Abd al-Qaadir al-Jilaani.

(g)   Q to Mahammad.

(h)   Short pious invocation.

(i)   Q as in (e).

(j)   Q as in (e).

(k)   Q as in (g).

(l)   Q as in (g).

(m)   Short pious invocation.

(n)   Q to Sh. Yuusuf al-Kawnayn.

(o)   Short pious invocation to Sh. Yuusuf al-Kawnayn.

(p)   Q as in (e).

(q)   Q as in (e).

(r)   Extr. m.: Draft of a private letter the subject of which is difficult to ascertain since its context is unknown.

(s)   Extr. m.: Draft of a legal testimony the subject of which is difficult to ascertain owing to partly illegible writing.

(t)   Extr. m.: Numerological calculations the nature of which is difficult to ascertain.

MS 7
2 pp. 16.3 x 20.5

(a)   Sh. Awat Wa'ays: Q to Sh. 'Isa, who is most probably the ancestor of the Somali clan family named after him.

(b)   Sh. 'Awat Wa'ays: Q as in (a).

MS 8
1p. 20.5 x 33.2

It is difficult to establish what the subject of this MS is. The text, which is illegible at several points, contains unconnected pious invocations, such as might be used in leather pouches worn as philacteries on arm or neck to protect against harm.

MS 9
2 pp. 20.5 x 33

Sh. 'Umar al-'Ayt: Q to Sh. Ibraahim al-Rashid.

An introductory note states that the author resides in Medina, while Sh. Ibraahim al-Rashid resides in Mecca. Probably both of them were either Arabs, or Somalis settled in Arabia.

MS 10
2 pp. 20.5 x 33

(a)   Sh. Mu'allim 'Abdi: Q to Sh. Qutub (fragment).

(b)   Sh. Mu'allim 'Abdi: Q as in (a).

MS 11
1 p. 20.5 x 33.2

A handwritten copy of the title page of *Majmuu'at qasaaid*, a printed work by Ibn Muhyi al-Din Qaasim al-Baraawe editor and co-author. The second edition of this book was published in Cairo in 1949. The date of the first edition is not known.

MS 12
1 p. 20.5 x 33.2

A sequence of pious invocations which may be such as are used in leather pouches worn as philacteries on arm or neck.

MS 13
1 p. 21 x 33.5

A poem composed in honour of I.M.Lewis's visit to Widhwidh.

MS 14
1 p. 20 x33.2

A list of books in MS form written by Sh. 'Ali Ibraahim. The books listed are collections of *qasidas* and prose works on religious subjects.

MS 15
2 pp. 16.3 x 20.5

   (a)   Sh. Aw Muusa: Q to Sayyid Ibraahim ibn Saalih.
   (b)   Extr. m.: An exercise in penmanship, consisting of groups of isolated words.

MS 16
1 p. 20.5 x 33

Q in praise of the Qaadiriyah *tariiqa*. The introductory note states that the poem contains a condemnation of the Saalihiya *tariiqa*, but that part of the text is missing.

MS 17
27 pp. 16.3 x 20.3

   (a)   Extr. m.: List of names without any indication of its purpose.
   (b)   Genealogy of Sh. Isaaq bin Ahmad.
   (c)   Extr. m.: Names of persons, numbers, isolated letters and a

diagram which are probably concerned with some form of numerological divination.

(d)   Q to a saint not identified by name. A description of the splendour of his annual pilgrimage feast suggests that it must be either Sh. Isaaq bin Ahmad or Sh. Yuusuf al-Kawnayn.

(e)   Q to Sh. Mahmuud Yaasin.

(f)   Q to Sh. Yuusuf al-Kawnayn.

(g)   Sh. 'Abd Khalif ibn Sh. Ahmad Nuur al-Din: Q to Muhammad.

(h)   Extr. m.: Sheep trade accounts.

MS 18
2 pp. 21.5 x 31.7

(a)   An account of a discussion between Sh. 'Abd Allaah bin Mu'allim Yuusuf al-Qutbi and Boqor 'Uthmaan Mahmuud about Sayyid Muhammad 'Abd Allaah Hasan. During it the sheikh strongly attacks the Sayyid's *fatwa* that those Somalis who had not joined him in the holy war against the Christians governing Somalia committed an act of apostasy and that it was then lawful to kill them.

(b)   Sh. 'Abd Allaah Mu'allim Yuusuf: A letter in poetic form addressed to the Sayyid. It was written after the Boqor had received a letter from the Sayyid seeking his friendship and alliance. Sh. 'Abd Allaah's letter to the Sayyid fiercely condemns his deeds and doctrines and accuses him of flagrant violations of Islamic Law and of apostasy.

MS 19
135 pp. 13.5 x 20

A handbook of Arabic grammar. The author is not stated but it was most probably composed by al-sheikh 'Abd al-Rahmaan bin Ahmad al-Zayla'i.

MS 20
47 pp. 20.5 x 32.5

(a)   Sh. 'Ali Sh. Ibraahim: Detailed hagiography of Sh. Isaaq bin Ahmad. It covers his life and deeds in the Arabian Peninsula and the Horn of Africa from his birth until the foundation of Mait town. The year of his death there is given as 727 AH. This hagiography contains an insert consisting of a eulogy of Sh. Isaaq by Adam bin 'Isa.

(b) Ahmad Nuuh (copied by 'Ali Jaama' Ibraahim): Q to Sh. Isaaq bin Ahmad. It contains a poetic description of a pilgrimage to the shrine of Sh. Isaaq at Mait.

(c) Sh. 'Umar bin Mahammad al-Maarisi (or Maarsi): Q to Sh. Isaaq.

(d) Sh. 'Umar bin Mahammad al-Maarisi (or Maarsi): Q as in (c).

(e) 'Umar bin 'Askar: Q as in (c).

(f) 'Ali bin Haajj Ibraahim: Q as in (c).

(g) 'Ali bin Haajj Ibraahim: Q as in (c).

MS 21
21 pp. 20.5 x 32.5

(a) Ahmad bin Ruublah: Q to Sh. 'Uthmaan bin Nuur.

(b) Taahir Ahmad 'Abdi: Hagiography of Sh. 'Uthmaan bin Nuur.

(c) Ahmad bin Ruublah: Q as in (a).

(d) Ahmad bin Ruublah: Q as in (a).

(e) Hagiography of Sh. 'Uthmaan bin Nuur, continued.

(f) Hagiographical note on an episode in the life of Sh. 'Abd al-Raaziq al-Dankali.

(g) Sh. 'Abd al-Raaziq al-Dankali: Q to Mahammad, composed on the occasion of the poet's miraculous release from an Ethiopian jail.

(h) Hagiographical notes on an episode in the life of Sh. 'Abd al-Raaziq al-Dankali.

(I) Sh. 'Abd al-Raaziq al-Dankali: Q to Mahammad composed on the occasion of the poet's miraculous cure from an illness.

(j) Hagiographical note on episodes in the life of of Sh. 'Abd al-Raaziq al-Dankali.

(k) Hagiography of Sh. Ibraahim Ahmad "Kabuulah".

(l) Sh. 'Abd al-Raaziq al-Dankali: Q to Sh. Ibraahim Ahmad "Kabuulah".

(m) Hagiography of Sh. Yuusuf al-Kawnayn.

(n) Yuusuf Muhammad bin al-Bakri: Q as to Sh. Yuusuf al-Kawnayn.

(o) Hagiography of Sh.Yuusuf al-Kawnayn, continued.

(p) General note on Somali Sufi *tariiqa*s and the veneration of saints.

(q) Hagiography of Sh. Mahammad bin Shirah, popularly known as Sh. Mahammad Yarah.

(r) Account of the state of Somali *tariiqa*s and the rise and disappearance of new *tariiqa*s, led by sheikhs who deviated from

Islamic orthodoxy or were downright fraudulent, in the period from 1940 to the first years after the end of the Second World War.

Although this is not explicitly stated it can be inferred from a note at the end of this MS that items (p) and (r) were written by Taahir Ahmad, whose nickname was 'Filsan', especially for this collection.

MS 22
21 pp. 20.5 x 32.5

(a) Biography of Sayyid Mahammad 'Abd Allaah Hasan.
(b) Description of the Saalihiya *tariiqa* and a hagiography of its founder, Sayyid Mahammad Saalih.

MS 23
14 pp. 20.5 x 32.5

(a) List of works of Sh. 'Abd al-Rahmaan bin Ahmad al-Zayla'i.
(b) Sh. 'Abd al-Rahmaan bin Ahmad al-Zayla'i. Hagiography of Sh. 'Abd al-Qaadir al-Jilaani.

MS 24
60 pp. 20.5 x 32.5

(a) Sh. Mahammad Huuruunah: Q to Sh. Isaaq bin Ahmad.
(b) Sh. Mahammad Huuruunah: Q as in (a).
(c) Sh. Yuusuf bin 'Abd Allaah: Q as in (a).
(d) Q to Mahammad.
(e) Q as in (a).
(d) Q as in (a).

MS 25
16 pp. 20.5 x 32.5

(a) The story of Sayyid Mahammad 'Abd Allaah Hasan and the Dervish War.
(b) Brief note on Somali poets.
(c) Brief notes on the Midjaan (Midgan), Tumal and Yibir occupational castes.
(d) Mahammad Sabri: Account of the Egyptian penetration of the Horn of Africa (this is most probably based on a published work by an Arab writer).
(e) Brief note about Somali starlore.
(f) Brief note on Somali traditional veterinary, medical and divinatory practices.

(g)   Description of Somali *tariiqa*s.

(h)   Brief note on pastoralism as the main concern of the Somali people.

MS 26
20pp. 20.5 x 32.5

(a)   Brief invocation to Sh. Mahammad, popularly known as Sh. Mad"ibaan, venerated by the people of the Midgan occupational caste as one of their Muslim saints. The symbol " in Mad"ibaan indicates that the Arabic letter *daal* in the original is written with three superscript dots corresponding to the diagraph dh in Somali orthography.

(b)   Extr. m.: Probably: Draft of an invitation to a fund-raising party.

(c)   Q to Sh. Mahammad (Sh. Mad"ibaan).

(d)   Q as in (c).

(e)   Q as in (c).

(f)   Q as in (c), but characterized by its deviation from the rules of Arabic versification.

(g)   Sh. Ibn Abaasi: Q to Sh. Muusa, venerated by the people of the Midgan occupational caste as one of their Muslim saints.

(h)   Q to Mahammad.

(i)   Q as in (f). In parts the text is identical with that of item (f).

(j)   Sh. Diriyah Bahar: Q as in (c), but written in Somali in Arabic characters. The transcription is very inadequate since it ignores the essential sound distinctions of Somali phonology.

MS 27
13 pp. 20.5 x 32.5

A legendary account of the wars conducted against the invasions of Muslim territories in the Horn of Africa by the Portuguese, Italians and Ethiopians. Sh. Abaadir, Sh. Yuusuf al-Kawnayn, Sh. Nuur Husseen of Bale and the Sultan of Mogadishu are principal figures in the narration. The account contains some anachronisms, such as putting Italian and Portuguese soldiers side by side and implying that they all arrived in a steamship.

MS 28
8 pp. 15 x 20

The pages are loose and come from a larger unidentified work.

They are severely damaged, probably by termites. The contents are in prose and consist of prayers, exhortations and affirmations of Islamic doctrine. It is difficult to ascertain what the unifying theme of the complete work was.

MS 29
1 p. 14.5 x 18.5
(a piece of cardboard)

This is an inscription of eight lines, found on the cover of a copy of the Koran in Berbera. It states that in 1319 AH a man called Mahad 'Abd Ismaa'il donated a gift to the 'Abd al-Qaadir Mosque. The gift appears to be a portion [of his land] and there are some explanations concerning the gift and the occasion for giving it but the text deviates so much from standard Arabic that it is difficult to establish its meaning with any certainty.

MS 30
4 pp. 9 x 14

(a)   Two pages which are severely damaged on the edges. The text is a fragment of *qasida* but is too short to suggest what its unifying theme is.

(b)   Two diagrams, probably connected with some divinatory practice.

MS 31
1 p. 20.5 x 33

Sh. 'Abd Allaah Majirtayn and Mahammad Hasan: A poem condemning the singing of love poems of the Somali *belwo* genre as offensive to Muslim morality and decorum.

Printed Pamphlets

PAM 1
8pp. 11.5 x 15

Ahmad bin Husayn bin Mahammad. 1945. *Manaaqib al-'Aarif bi-Allaah wa-al-daall 'alayhi, imaam al-Shariahh wa-fakhr al-haqiqah, al-Ustaadh al-Shaykh Ismaa'il bin Ibraahim al-Jabarti.* (The virtues and wondrous deeds of the man acquainted with Divine Knowledge and leader of others to God, imam of the Shariah, the pride of truth, Shaykh Ismaa'il bin Ibraahim al-Jabarti.) Cairo: Shirkat Maktabah wa-Matba'ah, Mustafa al-Baabi al-Halabi wa-Awlaaduhu.

PAM 2
11 pp. 11.5 x 15

Husayn bin Ahmad Darwish, al-Shaykh. 1375 AH *Amjaad.* (Glorious praises.) Aden: Al-Matba'ah al-'Arabiyah bin-Adan. [A hagiography of Sh. Isaaq bin Ahmad.]

BIBLIOGRAPHY

Abbreviations

AAE	Archivio per l'Antropologia e l'Etnologia (Florence)
AAI	Annali di Africa Italiana (Rome)
BSAI	Bolletino della Società Africana d'Italia
BSOAS	Bulletin of the School of Oriental and African Studies (London)
Enc. Is.	Encyclopaedia of Islam
GJ	Geographical Journal
JEANHS	Journal of the East African Natural History Society
JRAI	Journal of the Royal Anthropological Institute
JSA	Journal de la Société des Africanistes
RAL	Rendiconti della Reale Accademia dei Lincei (Rome)
REI	Revue des Études Islamiques
RC	Rivista Coloniale (Rome)
RETP	Revue d'Ethnographie et de Traditions Populaires
RSE	Rassegna di Studi Orientali (Rome)
RSO	Rivista degli Studi Orientali (Rome)
S. d. Ph.-Hist. Kl. D. K. Akad. D. Wiss.	
	Sitzungsberichte der Philosophisch-Historischen Klasse der Kaiserlichen Akademie der Wissenschaften (Vienna)
Z.f.Eing.Spr.	Zeitschrift für Eigneborenen Sprachen (Berlin)

ABBAS, HAJI, 'Le culte de Chaich Hussein dans l'Islam des Arsi, Ethiopia', in *Islam et Societés au Sud du Sahara*, 5,21-42, 1991.

ABDISALAN YASSIN MOHAMED, *Sufi Poetry in Somali: its Themes and Imagery*. Unpublished Ph.D. thesis, University of London (SOAS), 1977.

ABERRA KETSELA. *The Rebellion in Bale* (1931-1970). Unpublished B.A. dissertation, Haile Selassie University, Addis Ababa, 1971.

ALAWI ALI ADAN, 'A General Review of Somali Arabic Literature', in Hussein M. Adam and Charles L. Geshekter, (eds.) *Proceedings of the First International Congress of Somali Studies*. Atlanta, Georgia: Scholars Press pp. 299-314, 1992.

AMMAR, H, *Growing up in an Egyptian village*. London, Routledge and Kegan Paul, 1954.

ANDERSON, J. N. D. 'Homicide in Islamic Law', *BSOAS*, XIII, 4, 1951, 811-28.

____*Islamic Law in Africa*. (Colonial Research Publications, No. 16.) London, H.M.S.O. for the Colonial Office, 1954.

ANDRZEJEWSKI, B.W. and LEWIS, I.M. *Somali Poetry*, London, Oxford University Press, 1964.

ANDRZEJEWSKI, B.W. 'Allusive Diction in Galla Hymns in Praise of Sheikh Hussein of Bale', *African Language Studies*, XIII, 1-31, 1972.

____ 'Sheikh Hussein of Bale in Galla Oral Traditions' *Accademia Nazionale dei Lincei, IV Congresso Nazionale di Studi Etiopici*, 1, 463-479, 1974a.

____ 'The Veneration of Sufi Saints and its Impact on the Oral Literature of the Somali People and on their Literature in Arabic', *African Language Studies*, XV, 15-53, 1974b.

____ 'A Genealogical Note Relevant to the Dating of Sheikh Hussein of Bali', *BSOAS*, 38, 139-140, 1975.

____ 'Islamic Literature of Somalia', Fourteenth Annual Hans Wolff Memorial Lecture, African Studies Program, Indiana University. Bloomington 1983.

ARBERRY, A. J. *Sufism: an Account of the Mystics of Islam*. London, Allen and Unwin, 1950.

____*The Holy Koran: an Introduction with Selections*. London, Allen and Unwin, 1953.

BANTI, GIORGIO, 'Scrittura', in Annarita Puglielli, (ed.) *Aspetti del'espressione artistica in Somalia*. Rome: Università di Roma 'La Sapienza', pp. 19-29. 1987.

BARCLAY, H.B. *Buuri al-Lamaab*, Ithaca, New York, Cornell University Press, 1964.

BARILE, P. *Colonizzazione Fascista nella Somalia Meridionale*. Rome, 1935.

BARNES, J. A. *Politics in a changing society. A political history of the Fort Jameson Ngoni.* London, O.U.P. for the Rhodes-Livingstone Institute, 1954.

BAROJA, C.J. *Estudios Saharianos,* Madrid, 1955.

BASSI, M. *I Borana: Una società assembleare dell'Etiopia.* Milan: Franco Angeli, 1990.

BATTARA, P. 'Le osservazioni antropometriche eseguite dal Prof. A. Mochi in Eritrea', *AAE,* 66, 1934, 5-172.

BAXTER, P. 'Acceptance and Rejection of Islam among the Borana of the Northern Frontier District of Kenya', in I.M. Lewis (ed.) *Islam in Tropical Africa,* London, 233-252, 1966.

BELL, C. R. V. *The Somali Lanauage.* London, Longmans, 1953.

BERNARD, A., and MILLIOT, L. 'Les qânoûns kabyles dans l'ouvrage de Hanoteau et Letourneuz', *REI,* VII, 1933, 1-44.

BONO, E. 'La residenza di Bur Hacaba', *La Somalia Italiana,* 4, 5, 6, Mogadiscio, 3-23, 1929.

BOTTEGO, V. *Viaggi di Scoperta nel Cuore dell'Africa: il Giuba Esplorato.* Rome, 1895.

BRAUKAMPER, U. 'Islamic Principalities in South-east Ethiopia between the Thirteenth and Sixteenth Centuries', *Ethiopianist Notes,* 1, 1,2, 17-55; 1-44, 1977.

BRUNA, R. 'Monografia sulle popolazioni delle Acchele-Guzaui', *Relazione sulla Colonia Eritrea. Camera dei Deputati* (Rome), 32, 1907, 1,657-732.

BRYAN, M. A. *The distribution of the Semitic and Cushitic Languages of Africa.* London, O.U.P. for the International African Institute, 1947.

BURTON, Sir R. F. *First Footsteps in East Africa. Memorial edition.* London, 1894, 2 vols.

CAROSELLI, F.S. *Ferro e fuoco in Somalia,* Rome, 1931.

CASPANI, E., and Cagnacci, E. *Afghanistan, Crocevia dell'Asia.* Milan, 1951.

CASSANELLI, L. 1982, *The Shaping of Somali Society,* Philadelphia, University of Pennsylvania Press, 1982.

CERULLI, E. Article 'Zar' in *Enc, Is.,* IV, 1217.

____ 'Testi di diritto consuetudinario del Somali Marrehan', *RSO*, 7, 1918, 861-76.

____ 'Il diritto consuetudinario della Somalia Italiana Settentrionale', *BSAI*, 38, 1919, 93, pp. [Reprint.]

____ *The folk-literature of the Galla of Southern Abyssinia*. (Harvard African Studies, III) Cambridge, Mass., 1922

____ 'Note sul movimento Mulsulmano nella Somalia', *RSO*, 10, 1923, 1-36

____ 'Un gruppo Mahri nella Somalia Italiana', *RSO*, 11, 1926, 25-6.

____ 'Le popolazioni della Somalia nella tradizioni storica locale', *RAL*, ser. 6, II, 1926, 150-72.

____ 'Nuovi documenti arabi per la storia della Somalia', *RAL*, ser. 6, III, 1927, 392-410.

____ Le stazioni lunari nelle nozioni astronomiche dei Solai e dei Danakil', *RSO*, 12, 1929.

____ Tradizioni storiche e monumenti della Migiurtina', *AAI*, 4, 1-2, 1931. (1)

____ Nuovi appunti sulle nozioni astronomiche dei Somali', *RSO*, 13, 1931, 2-9. (2)

____ 'Le popolazioni del bacino superiore dello Uabi', in L. di Savoia, Duca degli Abruzzi, *L'Esplorazione dello Uabi-Uebi Scebeli*, Milan, 1931.

____ *Etiopia Occidentale*. Rome, 1933. 2 vols.

____ *Studi Etiopici. I. La Lingua e la Storia di Harar*. Rome, Istituto per l'Oriente, 1936.

____ *Studi Etiopici II: la Lingua e la storia dei Sidamo*, Rome, 1938.

____ Article 'Somaliland', *Enc. Is.*, IV, 483-8.

____ *Somalia. Studi editi ed inediti I*. Rome, 1957.

____ *Somalia. Studi editi ed inediti III*. Rome, 1964.

CHAMPARD, R. 'Notes sur quelques croyances religieuses des Galla', *RETP*, 1925, 125-35.

CHIODI, V. 'Gruppi sanguigni in relazione alla razza; loro possibile applicazione alla risoluzione dei problemi etnoantropologici riguardanti l'Africa Orientale Italiana', *AAE*, 67, 1934, 160-72.

CIPRIANI, L. *Abitazioni indigene dell'Africa Orientale Italiana*. Naples, 1940.

COLUNNI, M. *Principi di Diritto Consuetudinario della Somalia Italiana Meridionale*. Florence, 1924.

CONTI ROSSINI, C. 'Al-Ragali', *Boll. Soc. Ital. Di Espl. Geog.*, 193-4.

____ 'Schizzo del dialetto Saho dell'Alta Assaorta in Eritrea', *RAL*, 22, 5, 1913, 151-246.

____ 'Studi su popolazioni dell'Ethiopia: Gli Irob e le loro tradizioni', *RSO*, 3, 1914, 849-900.

____ 'Note sugli Agau', *Giornale Soc. Asiatica Italiana* (Florence), 1905, 17-8.

____*Etiopia e Genti d'Etiopia*. Florence. 1937.

CORNI, G. (ed.). *La Somalia Italiana*. Milan, 1937-8. 2 vols.

CUCINOTTA, E. 'Delitto, pena, e giustizia presso i Somali del Benadir', *RC*, 16, 1921, 15-41.

____ 'Proprieta', ed il sistema contrattuale nel ADestur@ Somalo', *RC*, 16, 1921, 243-64.

____ 'La costituzione sociale Somala', *RC*, 16, 1921, 442-56, 493-502.

CUNNISON, I.G. *Baggara Arabs*. Oxford: Clarenden Press, 1966.

CURLE, A.T. 'The Ruined Towns of Somaliland', *Antiquity*, 315-327, 1937.

DAINELLI, G., and MARINELLI, O. *Risultati Scientifici di un Viaggio nella Colonia Eritrea*. Florence, 1913.

DAUALIBI, M. *La Jurisprudence dans le Droit Islamique*. Paris, 1941.

DESCHAMPS, H. (ed.). *L'Union Française, Côte des Somalis-Réunion-Inde*. Paris, Berger Levrault, 1948, 1-85.

DRAGUE, G. *Esquisse d'Histoire Religieuse du Maroc*. (Cahiers de l'Afrique et l'Asie. II.) Paris, 1951.

DRAKE-BROCKMAN, R. E. *British Somaliland*. London, 1912.

DRYSDALE, J. G. S. 'Some aspects of Somali rural society to-day', *Somaliland Journal* (Hargeisa), I, 2, 1955.

ESHETU SETEGN. *Sheikh Hussein of Bale and his Followers*, unpublished

B.A. history dissertation, Haile Selassie University, Addis Ababa, 1973.

EICKELMAN, D. *The Middle East: an Anthropological Approach.* Englewood Cliffs: Prentis-Hall, 1981.

EVANS-PRITCHARD, E. E. *The Nuer.* Oxford, Clarendon Press, 1940.

_____ *The Sanusi of Cyrenaica.* Oxford, Clarendon Press, 1949.

_____ 'The meaning of sacrifice among the Nuer', JRAI, 84, 1954, 21-33.

FAKHRY, MAJID. 'The theocratic idea of the Islamic state in recent controversies', *International Affairs*, XXX, 1954, 450-62.

FEILBERG, C. G. *La Tente Noise.* Copenhagen, 1944.

FERRAND, G. *Les Çomalis: Matériaux d'études sur les pays Musulmanes.* Paris, 1903.

FERRANDI, U. *Lugh. Seconda Spedizione Bottego.* Rome, 1903.

FIRTH, R. 'Problem and Assumption in an Anthropological Study of Religion', *JRAI* 89: 129-148, 1959.

FORDE, D. (ed.) *African Worlds: Studies in the Cosmological Ideas and Social Values of African Peoples.* London, O.U.P. for the International African Institute, 1954.

FORTES, M. and EVANS-PRITCHARD, E.E. (eds.) *African Political Systems.* London, O.U.P. for the International Institute of African Languages & Cultures, 1940.

FREEDMAN, M. *Lineage Organization in South-East China.* London 1958.

_____ *Chinese Lineage and Society.* London 1966.

FYZEE, A. A. *Outlines of Muhammadan Law.* London, O.U.P., 1949.

GASTER, T. H. 'Myth and story', *Numen*, I, 1954, 184-213.

GIBB, Sir H. A. R. *Modern Trends in Islam.* Chicago, 1947.

_____ *Mohammedanism.* London, O.U.P., 1953.

_____ and BOWEN, H. *Islamic Society and the West.* Vol. I. London, O.U.P. for Roy. Inst. Internat. Affairs, 1950.

GOLDZIHER, I. Article *'Fikh', Enc. Is.,* II, 101-5.

GREENBERG, J. *The Influence of Islam on a Sudanese Religion*, Monographs of the American Ethnological Society, 10, New York, 1946.

GUILLAIN, C. *Documents sur l'histoire, la géographie, et le commerce de l'Afrique Orientale*. Paris, A. Bertrans, 1856. 3 vols.

HARRIS, G. 'Possession 'Hysteria' in a Kenyan Tribe', *American Anthropologist*, 59: 946-1066, 1957.

HELANDER, B. 'Notions of Crop Fertility in Southern Somalia', *Working Papers in African Studies*, 4, University of Uppsala, African Studies Programme.

_____ 'The Hubeer in the Land of Plenty: Land, Labour and Vulnerability Among a Southern Somali Clan', in C. Besteman and L.V. Cassanelli, (eds.) *The Struggle for Land in Southern Somalia*. Boulder & London, Westview Press & Haan, 1996.

_____ 'Rahanweyn Sociability: a Model for Other Somalis? In R.J. Hayward and I.M. Lewis, eds, *Voice and Power*. London: SOAS, 1996.

HUNT, J. A. *A General Survey of the Somaliland Protectorate, 1944-50*. London, Crown Agents for the Colonies, 1951.

HUNTINGFORD, G. W. B. *The Galla of Ethiopia: the Kingdoms of Kafa and Janjero*. (Ethnographic Survey of Africa. North-Eastern Africa, Part II.) London, International African Institute, 1955.

HURGRONJE, C. SNOUCK. *Mekka*. Haag, 1888-9. 2 vols. And atlas.

IBN KHALDÜN. Muqadimma' [trs. De Slane as] *Les Prolegomènes d'Ibn Khaldoun*. Paris, 1863-8. 3 parts.

JAHN, A. 'Lautlehre der Saho-Sprache in Nordabessinien', *Jahresbericht der K.K. StaatsRealschule* (Vienna), 23, 1909-10, 1-38.

JARDINE, D. *The Mad Mullah of Somaliland*, London, 1923.

JAUSSEN, A. *Coutumes des Arabes au Pays de Moab*. Paris, 1908.

KAHLE, P. 'Zr-Beschwörngen in Egypten', *Der Islam*, III, 1912, 1-41, 189-90.

LAMMENS, H. *L'Islam*. Beyrouth, 1944.

LA RUE, A. D. *La Somalie Française*. Paris, 1937.

LAURENCE, M. *A Tree for Poverty: Somali Poetry and Prose*. Nairobi, Eagle Press, 1954.

LEEUW, G. VAN DER. *Phänomenologie der religion*. Tübingen, 1933.

[Translated by J. E. Turner as *Religion in essence and manifestation*. London, 1938.]

LEIRIS, M. 'Le culte des Zrs à Gondar', *Aethiopias*, 4, 1934, 96-136. (1)

_____ *L'Afrique fantôme*, Paris, 1934, (2)

_____ *La possession et ses aspects theatraux chez les Ethiopiens de Gondar*, Paris, 1958.

LEWIS, B. *The Arabs in History*. London, 1950.

LEWIS, I. M. *The Social Organisation of the Somali*. MS. Thesis, Oxford B.Litt., 1953.

_____ *Peoples of the Horn of Africa: Somali, Afar [Danakil] and Saho*. (Ethnographic Survey of Africa. North-Eastern Africa, Part I.) London, International African Institute, 1955. London, Haan Associates, 1994.

_____ *The Somali Lineage System and the Total Genealogy*, Hargeisa, 1957.

_____ *A Pastoral Democracy*, London, Oxford University Press, 1961.

_____ *Marriage and the Family in Northern Somaliland*, East African Studies 15, Kampala, 1962.

_____ *The Modern History of Somaliland*, London, 1965.

_____ 'From Nomadism to Cultivation: the Expansion of Political Solidarity in Southern Somalia', in M. Douglas and P. Kaberry (eds.) *Man in Africa*, London, Tavistock, 59-78, 1969.

_____ *Ecstatic Religion*, Harmondsworth, Penguin Books, 1971.

_____ (ed.), *Symbols and Sentiments*, London, Academic Press, 1977.

_____ 'Literacy and Cultural Identity in the Horn of Africa: The Somali Case', in G. Baumann, (ed.) *The Written Word: Literacy in Transition*. Oxford: Clarenden Press, 1986.

LICATA, G. B. *Assab e i Danachili*. Milan, 1885.

LIENHARDT, G. *Divinity and Experience: The Religion of the Dinka*, Oxford, Clarendon Press, 1961.

LUCAS, M. 'Renseignements ethnographiques et linguistiques sur les Danakils de Tadjourah', *JSA*, 5, 1935, 182-202.

LULING, V. 'Notes on Possession Cults in the Mogadishu-Afgoi Area', London (unpublished), 1977.

MAINO, M. *Terminologia medica e sue voci nella lingua Somala*, Alexandria, 1953.

MARTIN, B.G. *Muslim Brotherhoods in Nineteenth Century Africa*. Cambridge: Cambridge University Press, 1976.

____ 'Shaykh Zayla'i and the Nineteenth Century Somali *Qaadiriya*.' In Said S. Samater, (ed.) *The Shadow of Conquest in Colonial Northeast Africa*. Trenton, NJ: The Red Sea Press, pp.11-32, 1992.

MASSIGNON, L. *Essai sut les origines de Lexique technique de la Mystique musulmane*. Paris, 1922.

____ Article *'Tarika'*, *Enc. Is.*, IV, 667-72.

____ Article *'Tasawwuf'*, *Enc. Is.*, IV, 681-85.

____ L'Umma et ses synonymes: notion de 'Communauté sociale en Islam', *REI*, [14,] années 1941-6, [pub.] 1947, 151-7.

MESSING, S. 'Group Therapy and Social Status in the Zar Cult of Ethiopia', *American Anthropologist*, 60: 1120-1127, 1958.

MILLIOTT, L. 'La conception de l'état et de l'ordre légal dans l'Islam', *Acad. De Droit International, Recueil des Cours*, 1949, II, 596-686.

____ *Introduction* a l'étude du droit Musulman, Paris, Recueil Sirey, 1953.

MOHAMMED, ALI Sheik. 'The origin of the Isaaq peoples', *Somaliland Journal* (Hargeisa), I, 1, 1954, 22-6.

MONTAGNE, R. *La civilisation du désert*. Paris, 1947.

MORENO, M. M. 'Problemi culturali della Somalia' *Africa*, VII, 9, 1952, 235-50.

____ M. *La Dottrina dell'Islam*. Bolgna, 1935.

____ *Il Somalo della Somalia*. Rome: Istituto Poligrafico dello Stato, 1955.

MUKHTAR, MOHAMED HAJI. 'Arabic Sources on Somalia', in *History in Africa, vol.14*, pp. 141-172, 1987.

____ 'Islam in Somali History: Fact and Fiction', in A.J. Ahmed (ed.) *The Invention of Somalia*. Lawrenceville NJ: The Red Sea Press, 1993.

NADEL, S. F. *Races and Tribes of Eritrea*. Asmara, Eritrea, British Military Administration, 1943.

____ 'A Study of Shamanism in the Nuba Hills', *JRAI* 76: 25-37, 1946.

____ *Nupe Religion*. London, 1954

NALLINO, C.A. *Raccolta di Scritti Editi e Inediti*. Vol.II. *L'Islam: Dogmatica-Sufismo-Confraternite*. Rome, Istituto per l'Oriente, 1940.

____ *Raccolta di Scriti Editi e Inediti*. Vol. IV *Diritto Musulmano,Diritti Orientali Cristiani*. Rome, Istituto per l'Oriente, 1942.

ODORIZZI, D. 'La Dankalia italiana de Nord', *Relazione sulla Colonia Eritrea. Camera dei Deputati* (Rome), 32 1907, 1,915-63.

PALERMO, G. M. DA. *Dizionario Somalo-Italiano e Italiano-Somalo*. Asmara, 1915.

PAULITSCHKE, P. *Beiträge zur Ethnogroaphie und Antrhopologie der Somal, Galla, und Harar*. Leipzig, 1880.

PETERS, E. *The Bedouin of Cyrenaica*. MS. Thesis, Oxford D.Phil., 1951.

POLLERA, A. *Le Popolazioni Indigene dell'Eritrea*. Bologna, 1935.

PUCCIONI, N. *Antropologia ed Etnologia delle Genti della Somalia*. Bologna, 1931-6. 4 vols.

____ *Le Popolazioni Indigene della Somalia Italiana*. (Manuali Coloniali.) Bologna, 1937.

RACHID, A. 'L'Islam et le droit des gens', *Acad. De Droit International, Recueil des Cours*. 1937, II, 371-506.

REINISCH, L. 'Die Afar Sprache', *S. d. Ph.-Hist. Kl. D. K.Akad. D. Wiss.* (Vienna), 111, 1886, 795-917; 114, 1887, 89-169.

____*Die Saho-Sprache*. Vienna, 1889-20. 2 vols.

____*Die Somali-Sprache*. Vienna, 1900-3. 3 vols.

ROBECCHI-BRICCHETTI, L. *Somalia e Benadir*. Milan, 1889.

RODWELL, J. M. (Tr.). *The Koran, translated from the Arabic*. London, Dent and Sons, 1909.

ROSS, A.D. 'Epileptiform Attacks Promoted by Music', *British Journal of Delinquency* 7: 60-63, 1956.

SAMATER, SAID S. *Oral Poetry and Somali Nationalism*. Cambridge: Cambridge University Press, 1982.

____ (ed.) *In the Shadow of Conquest: Islam in Colonial Northeast Africa*. Trenton, NJ: The Red Sea Press, 1992.

SANTILLA, D. *Istituzioni di Diritto Musulmano Malichita*. Rome, 1926-38. 2 vols.

SCHACHT, J. *The Origins of Muhammadan Jurisprudence*. Oxford, Clarendon Press, 1950.

___ Article '*Sharia*', Enc. Is., IV, 320-4.

SCHMIDT, W. *Der Ursprung der Gottesidee*. Bd. VII. Münster i. W., 1940.

SELIGMAN, C. G. *Races of Africa. First revised edition*. London, Thronton Butterworth, 1939.

SERGI, G. *Africa, Antropologia della stirpe Camitica*. Turnin, 1897.

SMITH, Sir W. Robertson. *Lectures on the religion of the Semites*. Edinburgh, 1889.

STEFANINI, G. *La Somalia, Noei e Impressioni di Viaggio*. Florence, 1924.

TASCHDJIAN, E. 'Stammenorganisation und Eheverbote der somalis', *Athropos*, 33, 1/2, 1938, 114-7.

THESIGER, W. 'The Awash River and the Aussa Sultanate', *GJ*, 85, 1935, 1-23.

TILING, M. von. 'Jabarti Texte', *Z.f.Eign.Spr.*, 15,1924/25, 50-64, 139-58.

TRIMINGHAM, J. S. *Islam in the Sudan*. London, O.U.P., 1949.

___ *Islam in Ethiopia*. London, O.U.P., 1952.

ULLENDORF, E. *The Semitic Languages of Ethiopia*. London, 1955.

VENIERI, L. 'Sull'etnografia dei Saho', *AAE*, 65, 1935, 5-59.

VERNAU, R. *Anthropologie et Ethnographie*. (Mission Duchesne Fournet en Ethiopie, Part II.) Paris, 1909.

WESTERMARCK, E. *Ritual and Belief in Morocco*, London, Macmillan, 1926.

WRIGHT, A. C. A. 'The interaction of various systems of law and custom in British Somaliland and their relation with social life', *JEANHS*, 17, 1-2, 1943, 66-102.

WÜSTENFELD, F. *Genealogische Tabellen der arabischen Stamme und Familien mit historische und geographischen Bemerkungen in einem alphabetischen Register*. Göttingen, 1852-3.

ZOLI, C. (ed.) *Notizie sul territorio della Riva Destra del Giuba, Oltre-Giuba*. Rome, 1927.

Index